Rogers M^cC

English II   1934-1935

SAMUEL TAYLOR COLERIDGE.

After a portrait painted in 1795.

The Academy Classics

THREE NARRATIVE POEMS

COLERIDGE: THE RIME OF THE ANCIENT MARINER
ARNOLD: SOHRAB AND RUSTUM
TENNYSON: ENOCH ARDEN

EDITED BY
GEORGE A. WATROUS, A.M.

REVISED BY
A. B. DE MILLE, A.M.
SIMMONS COLLEGE, BOSTON

—o•o—

ALLYN AND BACON

BOSTON   NEW YORK   CHICAGO
ATLANTA   SAN FRANCISCO

PTT

Norwood Press
J. S. Cushing Co. — Berwick & Smith Co.
Norwood, Mass., U.S.A.

PREFACE.

THE purpose of this volume of the *Academy Series* is to offer in a single book the three narrative poems set by the New York Regents for a part of second-year English. It is believed that the nature of the poems readily admits such grouping, and that the combination will be a convenience for teachers and a saving for students. Schools which offer only the reading required for entrance to college, and would therefore need only *The Ancient Mariner*, may find the present volume of advantage, in that its use will permit the student to make comparison with other narrative compositions. The text has been carefully chosen in each instance.

The editor gratefully acknowledges his obligations to other workers in the same field. The plan of the book is his own, but in the execution of that plan many sources have been freely drawn upon. The aim in the preparation of the notes has been to suggest to the student such other reading as will help him to interpret for himself the poem in hand. The map to make clear the geography of *Sohrab and Rustum* was made by Miss Alice Dertla Howes, to whom the editor would also acknowledge his gratitude for valuable suggestions embodied in the notes.

G. A. W.

UTICA FREE ACADEMY,
October, 1898.

PREFACE TO THE PRESENT EDITION.

SINCE the first edition of this book was published, twenty-five years ago, changes in the size of our public schools and in the type of pupils have created some difficult problems. The great increase of attendance throws a strain upon the library facilities which is not easy to meet. High school pupils of the present day engage in widely varied outside activities; many of them are disinclined to consult books of reference; others approach the study of literature with little or no background. In preparing a new edition of *Three Narrative Poems*, therefore, it seemed wise to increase the informational equipment. To this end, the lives of the poets have been entirely rewritten; the notes have been simplified and much enlarged; and a full list of practical topics has been added for use in oral and written work.

It is hoped that these revisions and additions will prove definitely helpful both to the general student and to those who are preparing for College Entrance Examinations.

A. B. DE M.

SIMMONS COLLEGE,
February, 1924.

CONTENTS.

LIST OF ILLUSTRATIONS.

INTRODUCTION.

SAMUEL TAYLOR COLERIDGE.

(1772–1834.)

SAMUEL TAYLOR COLERIDGE, the youngest of a large family, was born in a village of Devonshire, England, on

At Christ's Hospital. October 21, 1772. His father was a country clergyman in moderate circumstances, and welcomed the opportunity which came when the boy was ten years old to send him to a free school in London. This school was the famous Christ's Hospital[1]; widely known as the "Bluecoat School," from the uniform worn by the scholars. Here he spent about eight years, and suffered some hardships — though in little greater degree, probably, than was usual with the schools of the time.

He seems always to have been popular. Chief among his friends of those early days was Charles Lamb, afterwards the well-beloved author of the *Essays of Elia.*

Charles Lamb. Lamb was younger than Coleridge and from the first greatly admired his schoolmate, whom he describes as a "Logician, Metaphysician, Bard," and as "an inspired charity boy." The probability is that Coleridge already exercised those fascinating powers of conversa-

---

[1] Christ's Hospital was so named from one of the meanings of the Latin word *hospes*, a guest; a hospital, a place for those who needed shelter. It was founded by King Edward VI. (1547–1553) as a school for "the maintenance and education of a certain number of poor children born of citizens of London." The school occupied the original site in London until 1902, when it was moved to Sussex. In Coleridge's time there were about 700 boys.

tion which many years later led Carlyle to characterize him as "the most surprising talker extant in this world . . . to some small minority, the most excellent." The life at the school has been charmingly pictured in Lamb's familiar essay, *Christ's Hospital Five and Thirty Years Ago.*

Coleridge's school career ended in 1791, when he won an "Exhibition" Scholarship at Cambridge, and entered the University. Like a number of other great writers, he was not distinguished by any marked regard for academic requirements and never took a degree. He showed his intellectual capacity by winning the gold medal for a Greek ode in 1792, but thereafter the irresolution and lack of concentration which were the bane of his life became evident in everything he undertook. His interests turned uncertainly to poetry, to medicine, to metaphysics. At last he left the University secretly and went to London. Following a night in the streets, he enlisted in a regiment of dragoons, under the name of Silas Titus Cumberback. Of his military qualities there is little to be reported — he himself said that he hardly knew one end of a horse from the other — but he charmed his brothers-in-arms by his eloquence, and in some cases wrote their love-letters for them; surely a tribute to his genius. After a short time his friends secured his discharge and returned him to Cambridge. Soon, however, he left the University permanently, and went to Bristol.

Living in Bristol at the time was Robert Southey, whom Coleridge had met at Cambridge. The two young men renewed their acquaintance. It was the period when the French Revolution and the great changes incident thereto had filled the hearts of all generous youths with dreams of liberty, freedom, and equality — dreams that were recalled in the familiar passage written long afterwards by Wordsworth:

> "Bliss was it in that dawn to be alive,
> But to be young was very heaven, oh, times
> In which the meagre stale forbidding ways
> Of custom, law and statute, took at once
> The attraction of a country in romance."

The friends, stirred by the spirit of the day, but dowered with more enthusiasm than knowledge of the world, evolved a communistic system which they called "pantisocracy," and for the development of which they proposed to emigrate to America and found an ideal society on the banks of the Susquehanna. This fantastic scheme came to naught. Southey married, and changed his opinion as to the duties that lay before him; Coleridge married likewise, choosing the sister of Southey's wife. For a brief period he was settled and happy. But he was not destined either to peace or to happiness. He had become addicted to the use of opium, and from the effect of this habit as well as from the urge of his restless temperament he found it impossible to remain contented in the same environment for any considerable period.

At this stage in his career, when his mind "was filled with the chaos of a thousand visionary plans," he met the man who exercised upon him the strongest influence of his life. William Wordsworth, with his sister Dorothy, came to live in Somersetshire, in the south of England. Coleridge made their acquaintance and the three became close friends. Under the stimulus of this intimate association, which filled a need in Coleridge's nature that had never been satisfied before, he produced, between 1797 and 1802, the greatest

The Wordsworths.

work of his life. To these years belong *The Ancient
Mariner, Kubla Khan, Christabel, Osorio* — a tragedy
brought out later on in London under the name of *Remorse* — the *Ode to France*, the *Hymn to Sunrise*, and an
excellent translation of Schiller's *Wallenstein*.

The Wordsworths, for their part, were strongly drawn
to their brilliant young friend. "At first," writes Dorothy, "I thought him very plain; that is, for about three
minutes. He is pale, thin, has a wide mouth, thick lips,
and not very good teeth, longish, loose-growing, curling,
rough black hair. But if you hear him speak for five
minutes you think no more of them. . . . He is a wonderful man; his conversation teems with soul, and mind,
and spirit."

The outcome of the friendship between Coleridge and
Wordsworth was the publication in 1798 of *Lyrical Ballads*, one of the most important books that
" Lyrical   ever came from the press. We shall have
Ballads."   occasion to refer to it later. It was planned,
as Wordsworth says, to defray the expenses of a walking
trip among the Quantock Hills; the modest sum of £5 was
soon realized by its sale — though the volume brought
in little more than the amount desired.

William Hazlitt, one of the most interesting of English
Hazlitt's   critical writers, gives an estimate of the men,
Opinion.   both of whom he knew at this time :

"In the afternoon Coleridge took me over to Alfoxden, a romantic
old family mansion of the St. Aubins, where Wordsworth lived.
. . . Wordsworth himself was from home, but his sister kept house,
and set before us a frugal repast, and we had free access to her
brother's poems, the 'Lyrical Ballads,' which were still in man-
uscript. I dipped into a few of these with great satisfaction
and with the faith of a novice. . . ." Coleridge "lamented that

Wordsworth was not prone enough to belief in the traditional super-stitions of the place, and that there was a something corporeal, a matter-of-factness, a clinging to the palpable or often to the petty in his poetry, in consequence. We went over to Alfoxden again the day following, and Wordsworth read us the story of 'Peter Bell' in the open air. There is a *chant* in the recitation both of Coleridge and Wordsworth, which acts as a spell upon the reader and disarms the judgment. Perhaps they have deceived them-selves by making use of this ambiguous accompaniment. Col-eridge's manner is more full, animated, and varied; Wordsworth's more equable, sustained, and internal. Coleridge has told me that he himself liked to compose in walking over uneven ground, or breaking through the straggling branches of a copsewood, whereas Wordsworth always composed walking up and down a straight gravel walk, or in some spot where the continuity of his verse met with no collateral interruptions."

The story of Coleridge's life up to 1816 is a record of restless wandering. He traveled in Germany; he was **Restless Years.** for a time secretary to the Governor at Malta; he visited Rome; he strayed about various parts of England. In 1809 we find him at Grasmere, temporarily under the helpful influence of Wordsworth; in 1810 he forsook the Lakes and deserted his family, who were left to the care of the generous-hearted Southey. For the next few years "we can fol-low him but dimly." In 1813 Byron, then at the height of his popularity, used his great influence to bring out *Remorse* at Drury Lane Theater. About the same time Coleridge was lecturing in London on Shakespeare, Mil-ton, and the early dramatists. "I do hope," writes a friend, "he will have the steadiness to go on with the lectures to the end. It would be so great a point gained if he could but pursue one object without interruption. He surpasses himself," continues this friendly critic, "in the art of talking in a very interesting way without speaking at all upon the subject announced. . . . As evidence of splendid thought, and rare powers of expression and fancy, they are all that his hearers can wish; but as a discharge of his undertaking, a fulfillment of his promise to the public, they give his friends great uneasiness."

An end came, however, to this unhappy period. In 1816 Coleridge went to live with Dr. Gillman, at Highgate near London, and here he passed the remainder of his life. The Gillmans not only gave him the medical attendance which he sorely needed, but added the ministrations of a devoted friendship. Freed from the worst effects of his opium habit, he was able, as a recent writer puts it, to "make some salvage from the wreck." He wrote practically nothing — it was as a conversationist that he found mental activity — but he published several works that had been written before, and he collected and issued a complete edition of his writings.

Dr. Gillman.

Of Coleridge at this last stage of his career, when he had reached "port after stormy seas," some interesting accounts have come down to us. Charles Lamb, his life-long friend, spoke of him after his whimsical fashion as "an archangel, slightly damaged." But the truest, if not the most kindly, picture was drawn (as in so many other instances) by Carlyle. "Coleridge," he said, "sat on the brow of Highgate Hill in those years, looking down on London and its smoke-tumult like a sage escaped from the inanity of life's battle, attracting towards him the thoughts of innumerable brave souls still engaged there." He seems to have produced an effect of infinite capacity, not realizable in him-

The Closing Period.

self, but strong and helpful in the effect on other intelligences.   Carlyle again :

> "A sublime man ; who alone in those dark days had saved his
> crown of spiritual manhood ; escaping from the black material-
> isms and revolutionary deluges with 'God, Freedom, Immor-
> tality' still his ; a king of men.   The practical intellects of the
> world did not much heed him, or carelessly reckoned him a
> metaphysical dreamer ; but to the rising spirits of the young
> generation he had this dusky sublime character, and sat there as
> a kind of Magus, girt in mystery and enigma."

Of his personal appearance :

> "The good man, he was now growing old, towards sixty, per-
> haps ; and gave you the idea of a life that had been full of suffer-
> ings ; a life heavy laden, half vanquished, still swimming painfully
> in seas of manifold physical and other bewilderment.   Brow and
> head were round and of massive weight, but the face was flabby
> and irresolute.   The deep eyes of a light hazel were as full of
> sorrow as of inspiration ; confused pain looked mildly from them,
> as in a kind of mild astonishment."

His conversation was stimulating in a high degree, as many
have borne witness ; yet its manner — at least to the
clear and logical mind of Carlyle — was incoherent :

> "He began anywhere ; you put some question to him, made some
> suggestive observation ; instead of answering this, or decidedly
> setting out towards an answer of it, he would accumulate for-
> midable apparatus, logical swim-bladders, transcendental life-
> preservers, and other precautionary and vehiculatory gear for
> setting out ; perhaps did at last get under way — but was swiftly
> solicited, turned aside by the flame of some radiant new game on
> this hand or on that into new courses and ever into new. . . .
> Eloquent, artistically expressive words you always had ; piercing
> radiances of a most subtle insight came at intervals ; tones of
> noble pious sympathy were never wanting long."

Coleridge died at Highgate on July 25, 1834. None of his old friends was there at the last. Lamb felt the loss too deeply. "His great and dear spirit haunts me," he wrote afterwards. "Never saw I his likeness, nor probably the world can see again." Wordsworth broke down on learning of his death, calling him "the most *wonderful* man I have ever known."

At no time of his life — not even in his darkest hour — does there seem to have been any doubt of Coleridge's supreme poetic gifts. He was "an uncrowned king, carrying the seal of genius openly on his brow." Yet the sum total of the work which reveals his power is less than that of any other poet of the first rank. *The Ancient Mariner* and two or three other poems, some brilliant Shakespeare criticism, certain noble passages in the history of his thought which he called *Biographia Literaria* — these constitute his enduring titles to immortality. It is to the quality of his work that we must look if we would understand his unquestioned place in English poetry.

The quality is unique. In his greatest verse Coleridge was able to infuse the beauty of thought and expression with something higher,

> "to add the gleam,
> The light that never was on sea or land,
> The consecration, and the Poet's dream."

The phrase is Wordsworth's, and might well have been written of Coleridge, for the reader will find this indefinable trait in the magic of *The Ancient Mariner*, in the supernatural witchery of *Christabel*, or in that marvelous dream-fragment called *Kubla Khan*. His command of language was inimitable; his metrical form seemed to mold itself to the thought; his melody of diction has not been surpassed in literature. The exquisite little pictures of things familiar or imagined, which occur in the poems mentioned, show a felicity of imagery unlike anything we see elsewhere. His achievement was work of mystery and imagination, expressed in terms of the highest art. "Certain weaknesses in his character," says Professor Neilson, "prevented the world from reaping the full harvest of his marvelous intellect and imagination; yet in his best poems and criticisms we have a handful of masterpieces."

CHIEF WORKS OF SAMUEL TAYLOR COLERIDGE.

Moral and Political Lectures, 1795.
The Watchman, 1796.
The Rime of the Ancient Mariner (in *Lyrical Ballads*), 1798.
Translation of *Wallenstein*, 1800.
Remorse, 1816. (Originally named *Osorio*, and written in 1797.)
Kubla Khan, Christabel, etc., 1816.
  The former was written in 1797, the latter in 1801.
Biographia Literaria, 1817.
Sibylline Leaves, 1817. "Contains the whole of the author's poetical compositions, from 1793 to the present time."
The Poetical Works of S. T. Coleridge, 1829. An edition in three volumes, which was revised by the author himself.

MATTHEW ARNOLD.
(1822–1888.)

MATTHEW ARNOLD was born at Laleham in the county of Middlesex, England, in 1822. His father was the

Birth and Parentage. famous Dr. Thomas Arnold of Rugby School — the "Doctor" of *Tom Brown's Schooldays*. Dr. Arnold was one of the most remarkable figures of the nineteenth century in the educational world.

He took up his work at Rugby in 1828. The following words, written more than fifty years after his death, show what manner of man he was: "No one made a deeper change in education. As much as any one who could be named, Arnold helped to form the standard of manly worth by which Englishmen judge and submit to be judged. . . . A man of action himself, he sent out from Rugby men fit to do the work of the world. . . . Even in the volume of national life as it flows today, there may be detected the effect of the pure, bracing stream which long ago joined it." The influence of the father — "zealous, beneficent, firm" — is plainly to be traced in the life of the son; in his excellent work in the field of education and the undeviating loyalty of his writings to the highest standards of truth and justice.

Matthew Arnold was sent first to a private tutor at Laleham, and then at the age of thirteen to Winchester **Education.** School. A year later he was removed to Rugby, where he remained until he went up to Balliol College, Oxford, in 1841. His university career was a distinguished one. He gained the Newdigate Prize for his poem on Oliver Cromwell, won a scholarship, graduated with honors and in 1845 was made a Fellow of Oriel, the highest university distinction obtainable by an Oxford graduate. He moved in a brilliant circle of friends, chief among them being Arthur Hugh Clough, in whose memory he wrote the elegiac poem *Thyrsis*. "His perfect self-possession," writes one of these friends, describing the man at this time, "the sallies of his ready wit, the humorous turn which he could give to any subject which he handled, his gaiety, exuberance, versatility, audacity, and unfailing command of words, made him one of the

MATTHEW ARNOLD.

most popular and successful undergraduates Oxford has ever known." His own feeling for Oxford is well expressed in a familiar passage :

> "Beautiful city ! so venerable, so lovely, so unravaged by the fierce intellectual life of our century, so serene !
>
> 'There are our young barbarians, all at play.'
>
> And yet, steeped in sentiment as she lies, spreading her gardens to the moonlight, and whispering from her towers the last enchantments of the Middle Age, who will deny that Oxford, by her ineffable charm, keeps ever calling us nearer to the true goal of all of us, to the ideal, to perfection, — to beauty, in a word, which is only truth seen from another side ?"

After taking his degree, Arnold returned to Rugby where for a short time he taught classics. In 1847 he became secretary to Lord Landsdowne, a **Inspector of Schools.** position which he resigned in 1851 on receiving the important appointment of Inspector of Schools. This place he held until 1886 — two years before his death. There were few posts in the public service which offered a greater opportunity for influencing personally so large a number of people. While the work was not altogether congenial to him, he none the less developed its possibilities in a manner altogether strong and wise. One observer noted that his appearance in a school was like a ray of light when a shutter is suddenly opened in a darkened room, and that he was less interested in high marks than in happy children and sympathetic teachers. No small part of his influence was due to "his fine taste, his gracious and kindly manner, his honest and generous recognition of any new form of excellence which he observed."

The most far-reaching effect of his work is found in the

annual *Reports*, which attracted much public attention, and which are still worthy of study. He insisted, for instance, upon the need of including in the course of even elementary schools some "formative" ingredients — that is, studies (such as poetry) which had no immediate bearing upon the industrial career of the pupils. He further held that the competent instructor should broaden his outlook on life by personal cultivation. "The teacher," says the *Report* of 1878, "will open the children's soul and imagination the better, the more he has cleared his own." These words would serve as sound doctrine at the present time.

His educational duties involved several visits to the Continent as commissioner to study European methods. At various times he reported upon schools in France, Holland, Switzerland, Italy, and Germany. Such points as the following were taken under consideration : free education, quality of education, training and pensions of teachers, compulsory attendance, and release from school. His investigations were always carried out in thorough fashion ; and although his *Reports* — which were afterwards published as separate books — have today chiefly an historical interest, yet they formed at the time of their appearance a most useful body of educational theory.

Commissioner.

Like several of his famous contemporaries, Arnold went to the United States to lecture. He was not anxious for the experience, "I don't like going," he said. "I don't like lecturing. I don't like living in public, and I wish it was well over. I shall be glad, however, to see an American common school with my own eyes." He gave two lecture courses in this country, in 1883 and 1886, and a summary of his impressions and his

In America.

lectures may be found in his collected works — *A Word More about America, Discourses in America,* and *Civilization in the United States.*

His busy and useful life ended suddenly in 1888. He died at Liverpool, and was buried in Laleham churchyard.

Death. Besides his success in the field of education, Arnold won high rank as a poet, and was among the most distinguished critics of the nineteenth century.

His first volume of verse, *The Strayed Reveller and Other Poems,* appeared in 1848. It was soon followed by two more collections, the latter of which was pub-

Arnold as Poet. lished in 1853, under the title of *Poems by Matthew Arnold, a New Edition,* and brought him the fame that he deserved. Among the poems included were *Sohrab and Rustum,* considered by many to be the author's masterpiece; *The Scholar-Gypsy;* and the exquisite little lyric, *Requiescat.* The preface to this volume was of great importance, because it stated Arnold's theory of the poetic art. Some of the points which he established, in this and other writings on the subject, may be mentioned. The best poetry must possess a "high seriousness," in its aim and its expression; form and matter are equally important and must receive equal consideration; "the value of a poem consists more in the force and truth of the total impression, than in isolated fine thoughts sparkling forth in the heat of composition."

His theories were consistently exemplified by his own work, and his critical opinions were listened to with the

Theory and Practice. more respect because of the fine quality of his poetry. In none of his poems, perhaps, are these theories more fully illustrated than in *Sohrab and Rustum.* "The Poet," he said in the 1853

Preface, "has in the first place to select an excellent action; and what actions are the most excellent? Those, certainly, which appeal most powerfully to the great primary human affections: to the elementary feelings which subsist permanently in the race and which are independent of time." Nothing could appeal more strongly to the emotions than the involuntary death of a son at the hands of his father; while the poem possesses that high seriousness, simplicity of form, and unity of total impression which were the canons of Arnold's art. The wisdom of his theory and the excellence of his practice led to his appointment in 1857 as Professor of Poetry at Oxford. This position he held for ten years, though after 1860 he wrote little poetry. It was at Oxford, during this time, that much of his best critical work was done.

In his prose Arnold attains a confident attitude towards life; but his poetry frequently reflects the intellectual struggle through which he passed. Many of **His Poetic Note.** his poems are conceived in a mood of doubt. But however keen his scepticism may be, we are always conscious of the mind of a seeker after truth who is brave, honest, and sincere. Thus, even when their thought is pessimistic, the poems are to those who understand them aright a help and a stimulus. A few of the most typical may be suggested here. They are: *Dover Beach*, *A Summer Night*, and *Philomela; Shakespeare; Rugby Chapel*, the noble lines in memory of his father; *Geist's Grave*, *The Forsaken Merman*, and *Isolation*. In all his poetry he teaches firmness in meeting that which we cannot understand, courage in the face of the inevitable. Some lines from *The Better Part* may be taken to epitomize his thought:

"Hath man no second life? *Pitch this one high!*
Sits there no judge in Heaven, our sin to see?
More strictly, then, the inward judge obey!
Was Christ a man like us? *Ah, let us try*
If we then, too, can be such men as he!

The least successful part of his poetry was his dramatic work. He wrote three dramas, following with great fidelity the Greek models. They were named: **Dramas.** *The Strayed Reveller, Empedocles on Etna,* and *Merope.* But his genius was not adapted to this form of art. The poems contain some brilliant passages and some beautiful nature pictures, but they fail in the essentials — in plot, in character-drawing, and in the effective control of action.

Most of Arnold's poetry, as we have seen, was written before he was forty; his work in prose criticism began in 1861 with the publication of his lecture **Arnold as Critic.** *On Translating Homer.* This was the first step in the conscious effort, continued throughout his life, to create higher standards both in thinking and in living. In presenting his ideas, he used what has been termed the method of criticism; that is, he developed his thesis by comment, by suggestion, by persuasion. Criticism was defined by him as "the disinterested endeavor to know and propagate the best that has been thought and said in the world." To know the best in literature, one must make use of "touchstones" drawn from the great writers of the past; only by a knowledge of the best can the mind be freed from narrow views and false judgments. To attain the best in life, one must seek culture — the "ideal of all-round perfection, of sweetness and light." The style in which these ideas are

formulated is singularly lucid and urbane; it is sometimes marked by a pleasant kind of incisive irony which
is very effective. Repetition is frequently employed to
drive home a point, as may be seen in this passage about
the Greek poets:

> "No other poets have lived so much by the imaginative reason;
> no other poets have made their works so well balanced, no other
> poets have so well satisfied the thinking power; have so well
> satisfied the religious sense."

While his works were concerned primarily with problems
of the time, yet they contain much of permanent value.

Views on Literature and Life. The *Essays in Criticism*, published in 1865, placed
him among the greatest contemporary essayists.
At first, as in this volume, the subjects that attracted him were literary. He laid down principles of
sound judgment and canons of good taste which were well
illustrated by the classical dignity and simplicity of his
own best work. But his conclusion that the highest type
of poetry must be a "criticism of life" came to imply not
only artistic appeal but the deeper questions of ethics and
morality. Thus, in *Culture and Anarchy*, which appeared
in 1869, he attacked the narrowness and the false standards of his fellow-countrymen, and pointed the way to
higher ideals in life and thought. Other books which
followed — *Friendship's Garland, Literature and Dogma, God
and the Bible* — carry on the fight against the weaknesses
which he deplored in society, in politics, and in religion.

Culture is a word that has come to have some unfor-
tunate connotations; but with Arnold it signified nothing

"Culture." less than "the measure of the stature of the
perfect man"; it embodied perfection, not
only in things literary, but in all the varied relations of

life. The reader of the present day finds a great deal that is timely, as well as stimulating, in the high thought and lucid expression of Arnold's prose.

The personal qualities of Matthew Arnold are justly estimated in the words of one who knew him well:

> "He was most distinctly on the side of human enjoyment. He conspired and contrived to make things pleasant. Pedantry he abhorred. He was a man of this life and the world.
>
> **An Estimate.** A severe critic of this world indeed he was; but, finding himself in it, and not precisely knowing what is beyond it, like a brave and true hearted man, he set himself to make the best of it. Its sights and sounds were dear to him. The 'uncrumpling fern, the eternal moonlit snow,' the 'red grouse springing at our sound,' the tinkling bells of the 'high-pasturing kine,' the vagaries of men, of women, and dogs, their odd ways and tricks, whether of mind or manner, all delighted, amused, tickled him.
>
> "In a sense of the word which is noble and blessed, he was of the earth earthy. His mind was based on the plainest possible things. What he hated most was the fantastic — the far-fetched, all-elaborated fancies, and strained interpretations. He stuck to the beaten track of human experience, and the broader the better. This is his true note."

This view may be supplemented by the opinion of John Morley, historian, critic, and discriminating friend:

> "He was incapable of sacrificing the smallest interest of anybody to his own; he had not a spark of envy or jealousy; he stood well aloof from all the hustlings and jostlings by which selfish men push on; he bore life's disappointments — and he was disappointed in some reasonable hopes — with good nature and fortitude; he cast no burden upon others, and never shrank from bearing his own share of the daily load to the last ounce of it; he took the deepest, sincerest, and most active interest in the well-being of his country and his countrymen."

CHIEF WORKS OF MATTHEW ARNOLD.

Poetry :

The Strayed Reveller, and Other Poems, 1849.

Poems, 1853.

This volume contained the famous Preface on poetry. Among the poems were *Sohrab and Rustum, Requiescat,* and *The Scholar-Gypsy.*

Merope; a Tragedy, 1858.

New Poems, 1867.

Among the poems were *Dover Beach, Rugby Chapel,* and *A Southern Night.*

Thyrsis, 1866.

Prose :

Essays in Criticism, 1865.

Culture and Anarchy, 1869.

Friendship's Garland, 1871.

Literature and Dogma, 1873.

Discourses in America, 1885.

Essays in Criticism, Second Series, 1888.

ALFRED, LORD TENNYSON.
(1809–1892.)

ALFRED TENNYSON, the most representative and most popular poet of the nineteenth century, was born in August 1809 at the village of Somersby, Lincolnshire. In a family of twelve children he was the third of eight brothers, two of whom besides himself showed poetic genius. His early training was received chiefly from his father, a man of exceptional gifts and strongly marked characteristics. During his boyhood he gave some indication of the great powers which afterwards developed. When still very young, he wrote a poem on the death of his grandmother, for which he received from his grandfather the present of

Early Years.

ALFRED, LORD TENNYSON.

half a sovereign ($2.50) with the remark : "That is the first money, my boy, you've made by poetry, and, take my word for it, it will be the last." At the age of twelve he composed a long epic in imitation of Scott, with which his father was much impressed. "If that boy dies," said he, "one of our greatest poets will have gone."

Such early experimenting led to a poetical venture with his brother Charles, a little volume called *Poems by Two Brothers*, published in 1826. Their aim was pocket-money; poetic fame was a secondary consideration. The proceeds were spent on a tour round the churches of Lincolnshire. The poems were not marked by any special promise of future achievement; they did manifest, however, an unusual freedom from youthful crudities.

Alfred and Charles went up to Cambridge in 1828 and entered at Trinity College. Life at the University influenced the poet through the men he met and the
University Career. friends he made more than through academic opportunities. There gathered about him as time went on a brilliant group of undergraduates, a number of whom afterwards won fame in various walks of life. His closest friend was Arthur Henry Hallam, son of the great historian. A man of high attainments, his influence upon Tennyson's career was strongly marked. In his memory was composed the poem *In Memoriam*, one of the author's greatest works. During the autumn of 1830, the two went to Spain to help the revolutionists in their struggle for freedom. "A wild time we had of it," said Hallam; "I played my part as conspirator in a small way." Nothing much was accomplished, however, except as the experience formed an outlet for the typical spirit of generous youth.

The growing poetic power of Tennyson was shown by his winning the Vice-Chancellor's medal in 1829 with his poem *Timbuctoo*, which in the opinion of good critics manifested distinct promise. Later, in the year of the Spanish visit, he published his first independent volume — *Poems, chiefly Lyrical.* A volume by his brother Charles was issued about the same time, and the young authors must have been highly gratified by the testimony of Wordsworth : "We have a respectable show of blossom in poetry — two brothers of the name of Tennyson ; one in particular not a little pleasing." Upon the death of his father in 1831, Tennyson left the university without proceeding to a degree.

His next book, *Poems* (1832) may fairly be considered the precursor of a new school of poetry. Its charm of
Poems, 1832.
diction and the highly "decorative" beauty in which its thoughts were clothed were typical of the Tennysonian style and plainly showed the trend of his genius. They revealed fresh and unsuspected possibilities of English verse. Among the poems in the collection were *The Lady of Shallot, The Lotus-Eaters, A Dream of Fair Women,* and *The Palace of Art.* Charles Dickens was especially impressed by the lines from *A Dream of Fair Women:*

> "Squadrons and squares of men in brazen plates,
>   Scaffolds, still sheets of water, divers woes,
>   Ranges of glimmering vaults with iron grates,
>   And hushed seraglios."

"What a relief," he cried, "in these days to come upon a man who can *write!*" The remark may stand as an epitome of the opinion of discerning readers, for many felt that here at last was a worthy successor in the line of the great English poets. On the other hand, some authorities handled the book severely, the criticism of the Edinburgh *Quarterly* being especially harsh.

Tennyson was always sensitive to adverse criticism — though he usually profited by it — and the effect in this case was strong. About the same time, in Ten Silent Years. 1833, he also suffered the great grief of his life. Arthur Hallam his best-loved friend, died at Vienna, whither he had gone in quest of health. For ten years the poet suffered much from depression of spirits, and published nothing. He lived chiefly in London during these "silent years." But the time was by no means lost, for there he met Carlyle. The influence of the great Scotchman is to be traced in the graver and more philosophic spirit of the later poems — more particularly *In Memoriam.* Carlyle himself found in Tennyson "a true human soul, or some approximation thereto, to whom your own soul can say, Brother!"

From his clear insight comes this memorable picture:

"A great shock of rough, dusty-dark hair; bright, laughing, hazel eyes; massive aquiline face, most massive, yet most delicate; of sallow brown complexion, almost Indian-looking; clothes cynically loose, free and easy; smokes infinite tobacco. His voice is musically metallic — fit for loud laughter and piercing wail, and all that may lie between; speech and speculation free and plenteous; I do not meet in these late decades such company over a pipe. We shall see what he will grow to."

The period of silence ended in 1842 with the publication of *Poems* in two volumes, the first principally composed of poems which had already appeared, the second entirely new. Among the new poems were *Ulysses, Locksley Hall, The Vision of Sin,* and *Morte D'Arthur.* Their indubitable qualities of beauty and strength set the seal upon his reputation, and caused Wordsworth to write: "He is decidedly the first of our living poets."

Tennyson always referred to the year 1850 as "Annus Mirabilis" — the wonderful year — and he had good reasons for doing so. It was marked by the publication of *In Memoriam*, in some respects his greatest poem; his marriage to Emily Sellwood; and his appointment to the office of Poet Laureate. The post had fallen vacant upon the death of Wordsworth, and the choice of the Government met with universal approval. The year marked, moreover, the beginning of almost unbroken happiness and good fortune. To very few writers has it been given to enjoy continuous critical and popular approval, and to retain to the last the full enjoyment of intellectual and artistic powers.

The "Annus Mirabilis."

We must not forget, however, that with his supreme poetic gifts was combined a strongly "human" personality. Indeed, the charm of his companionship was to those who knew him quite equal to the delight of his poetry. Retiring as was his disposition naturally, he nevertheless had friends in all walks of life, owing without doubt to his sincerity and his sympathetic breadth of mind. Besides the noteworthy comment of Carlyle, we have other interesting sidelights on the poet at various stages of his career. "It is very possible," writes a friend in 1842, "you may come across him in a country inn, with a foot on each hob of the fireplace, a volume of Greek in one hand, his meerschaum in the other, so far advanced towards the seventh heaven that he would not thank you to call him back to this nether world."

Friends.

The American poet Bayard Taylor stayed with him at

Farringford in 1857. "I was struck," he says, "by the variety of his knowledge. Not a little flower on the downs escaped his notice, and the geology of the coast, both terrestrial and submarine, was perfectly familiar to him. I thought of a remark I once heard from a distinguished English author (Thackeray), that Tennyson was the wisest man he knew." Speaking of his personal appearance, Taylor wrote that he was "tall and broad-shouldered as a son of Anak, with hair, beard, and eyes of Southern darkness." Hawthorne thought him "as un-English as possible," yet not American ; "I cannot well describe the difference, but there was something more mellow in him, softer, sweeter, broader, more simple than we are apt to be."

As we have seen, *In Memoriam* appeared some seventeen years after the death of the friend whose death it com-
memorates. During the intermediary period the poem developed from a personal lament to a broadly philosophic expression of the great issues of faith and doubt, and the supreme questions of death and immortality. In form it is a series of beautiful lyrics unified by the solemn central theme. Tennyson said: " It is rather the cry of the whole human race than mine. In the poem altogether private grief swells out into thought of and hope for the whole world. It begins with a funeral and ends with a marriage, begins with death and ends with promise of new life. . . . It is a very impersonal poem, as well as personal. There is more about myself in *Ulysses*, which was written under the sense of loss and all that was gone by, but that life must still be fought out to the end." The whole is a sort of soul-history, through sorrow and despair to sanity and

In Memoriam.

hope; a progress not unlike the experience recorded in Carlyle's *Sartor Resartus.*

Two other of the longer poems — *The Princess* and *Maud* — were published respectively in 1847 and 1855. The former is a treatment half serious and half fantastic of the place of woman in the modern world. It contains

The Prin-
cess, and
Maud.

passages of great beauty, and some songs which are among the most charming in the language.

In so far as any solution of the problem is offered (and the poem is an amusing tale altogether apart from the problem involved), it is offered by "emphasizing for us the laws of nature which determine in their inexorable fashion the place of man and the place of woman in any social system which is to endure."

Maud is a monodrama; that is, it represents the varying moods of a single character. As its author said, successive phases of passion in one person take the place of successive persons. It contains the expression of some of his strong feelings; the lyrics scattered throughout show him at his best; it was, taken all in all, his favorite poem. "I've always said," was his own comment, "that *Maud* and *Guinevere* were the finest things I've written."

Best known of all his writings, perhaps, are the *Idylls of the King.* The stories of King Arthur and his Knights

Idylls of
the King.

of the Round Table comprise the most important body of myth and legend in English annals, and they early attracted his attention. *The Lady of Shalott* appeared in 1832. The general subject, once revolved in his mind, strongly aroused and engaged his interest. By 1859 he published the first collection of *Idylls* — *Guinevere, Enid, Vivien,* and *Elaine;* the fragment called *Morte D'Arthur,* which determined the metrical form of the whole series, had been included in the *Poems* of 1842. Other *Idylls* were written at intervals up to 1888; by that time the entire group, having undergone many changes and revisions both in title and form, assumed the shape in which we know them today.

In their final form the *Idylls* comprise a group of twelve narrative poems loosely bound together by their general relation to the Arthurian legend. Broadly **Final Form.** speaking, they tell of the coming of the King, the destruction of wrong and oppression throughout his realm, the gradual appearance of evil among his knights, the "last great battle in the West," and the passing of Arthur to the "island valley of Avilion." At the same time, each *Idyl* is complete in itself, and the whole poem approximates the epic type. But Tennyson himself knew that the finished work did not possess the unity conferred by one strong central figure, as is characteristic of epic poetry. Hence, he chose a title which indicates the nature of what he tried to do. The result of his long endeavor was not an epic in the true sense of the word; it was rather a presentation of a group of noble episodes, a series of pictures of the high glory of past legend, of

> "old, forgotten, far-off things,
> And battles long ago."

But this is by no means all that he aimed at. Behind the beauty of the poetry, the richness of the imaginative treatment, the loftiness of the thought, is a **The Allegory.** deeper meaning. The story is "new-old, and shadowing Sense at war with Soul." Of the complete work, Tennyson said: "The whole is a dream of man coming into practical life and ruined by one sin. Birth is a mystery, and death is a mystery, and in the

midst lies the table-land of life, and its struggles and per-
formance." The allegorical element is seen especially in
The Coming of Arthur and *The Holy Grail*. It must be considered, however, as subsidiary to the narrative. The *Idylls*
are fascinating tales, and to the average reader their chief
interest will always lie in their romantic treatment of men
and events, the beauty of their background of mediæval
chivalry, and the fine perfection of their technical form.

The various phases of English country life interested
Tennyson at all times, and he wrote a number of poems
which he termed English Idylls. They differ
The Eng-
lish Idylls. widely from the *Idylls of the King*, chiefly
in their simplicity. They have a quiet and
characteristic charm. Among the best are : *Enoch Arden*,
which is dealt with at length in another place ; *Dora, The
Brook*, and *The Miller's Daughter*. To compare these
vignettes of real life with the philosophic thought of *In
Memoriam*, the spirit of revolt depicted in *Maud* or *Locksley Hall*, or with the confession of faith found in *The
Ancient Sage*, is to gain an adequate idea of the range of
Tennyson's power.

About the year 1875, Tennyson became interested in
the composition of dramas. For a considerable period
this form of poetry deeply engrossed him.
The Dramas. But the result was not happy. His versatility
was immense, and in every other poetic field he won success ; here, he could not command it. Between 1875 and
1884 he wrote a number of plays. Among them may be
mentioned *Harold, Becket*, and *Queen Mary*, touching
upon great epochs of English history, and *The Foresters*,
a woodland drama founded on the Robin Hood legends.
None of them, however, was marked by sufficient drama-

tic quality to hold the stage. Effective and beautiful in their language and their descriptive passages, they revealed no striking power of characterization, no command of conversational brilliancy.

The one gain from his experimenting in dramatic form was seen in some noble dramatic lyrics, in which his strong individualism and his sense of the picturesque enabled him to produce memorable effects. This is evident in the *Ballads* of 1880, where the dramatic feeling is expressed in a form wholly suited to his genius. We have the stirring appeal of ballads like *The Revenge* and *The Defence of Lucknow*, the grim pathos of *Rizpah* and *The Sisters*.

The later poems, contained in *Tiresias* (1885), and *Demeter* (1889), show no trace of the intellectual deterioration which so often is the sad accompaniment of old age. The high seriousness of

Lost Poems.

their outlook on life, and the full rich music of their verse, manifest the same noble qualities, set to a more solemn key, that had characterized the poet through all his long career. He died at Aldworth on October 6, 1892, crowning like his own Geraint, "a happy life with a fair death." At the time there was actually in the press his last volume — *The Death of Oenone, Akbar's Dream, and Other Poems*. In these poems the aged poet speaks of the meaning of life, the significance of death, of the need for a "faith beyond the forms of faith." Some lines from *God and the Universe* may well stand as his final message to the world:

"Spirit, nearing yon dark portal at the limit of thy human state,
Fear not thou the hidden purpose of the Power which alone is
    great,
Nor the myriad world, his shadow, nor the silent Opener of the
    Gate."

One or two other matters remain to be recorded. Tennyson had two places of residence after his marriage. One was the comfortable house at Farringford on the Isle of Wight, which he was very fond of and which is commemorated in the lines,

> " . . . far from noise and smoke of town,
>   I watch the twilight falling brown
>   All round a careless order'd garden
>   Close to the ridge of a noble down. . . .

> " For groves of pine on either hand,
>   To break the blast of winter, stand ;
>   And further on, the hoary Channel
>   Tumbles a billow on chalk and sand."

After 1867 he reserved Farringford for the winter, and spent the summer and autumn at Aldworth in Surrey, where he built a beautiful home — " a handsome and commodious house," one of his visitors called it, " in a most inaccessible place." A very practical recognition of his literary fame was the peerage offered to him by Gladstone, at the time Premier, as a mark of the national esteem. He accepted the honor, somewhat reluctantly, in 1883.

The most touching tribute to Tennyson was that written by his friend and fellow-artist, Robert Browning. It was voiced in a letter written just before his **Browning's Tribute.** own death in 1889, on the occasion of the Laureate's eightieth birthday :

" My dear Tennyson : Tomorrow is your birthday, indeed a memorable one. Let me say I associate myself with the universal pride of our country in your glory, and in its hope that for many and many a year we may have your very self among us — secure that your poetry will be a wonder and delight to those appointed to come after. And for my own part, let me further say, I have loved you dearly. May God bless you and yours."

CHIEF WORKS OF ALFRED TENNYSON.

Poems by Two Brothers, 1826.
Poems, 1832.
Poems, 1842.
The Princess; a Medley, 1847.
In Memoriam 1850.
Maud, 1855.
Idylls of the King, 1859.
  (Published in final form, 1888.)
Enoch Arden, 1864.
Queen Mary: a Drama, 1875.
Harold: a Drama, 1876.
Ballads and Other Poems, 1880.
The Promise of May: a Drama, 1882.
Becket, 1884.
Tiresias, and Other Poems, 1885.
Locksley Hall Sixty Years After, 1886.
Demeter, and Other Poems, 1889.
The Foresters, a romantic pastoral play, 1892.
The Death of Oenone, 1892.

A NOTE ON NARRATIVE POETRY.

Poetry is usually divided into three classes: Lyric, Dramatic, and Narrative. Lyric poems deal in an emotional way with a single thought, feeling, or situation, and are generally short. Dramatic poetry comprises the great body of verse written primarily for presentation on the stage. Narrative poetry embraces the large group in which story-telling is the chief consideration. It has four divisions — the *ballad*, the *epic*, the *romance*, and the *tale*.

Classes of Poetry.

The ballad is a poem which tells a story in the simplest way. Ballads flourished principally in the fourteenth and fifteenth centuries. The early examples —
The Ballad. such as *Sir Patrick Spens, The Wife of Usher's Well,* and the *Robin Hood* cycle — were anonymous. They were characterized by extreme simplicity of thought and diction, and by certain elements of the grim and the pathetic. Later came ballads of known authorship showing a more conscious art — *Tom Bowling, Sally in Our Alley, Lord Ullin's Daughter, La Belle Dame Sans Merci,* etc. In these the ballad simplicity persists, and there is found frequently the grim or the pathetic note which is equally characteristic.

When Coleridge wrote *The Ancient Mariner,* he deliberately chose the ballad form as best suited to his story.
The Ancient Mariner. It has all the marks of the true ballad: the simple metrical structure (modified now and again), the straightforward narrative method, the grim or pathetic touches. Coleridge added, of course, his own contribution — great melodic charm, and nature pictures of wonderful beauty. But in all essentials his poem is characteristic, and is one of the best illustrations of the type.

The epic is a long poem, written in stately verse and dealing with episodes in the life of some god, hero, or
The Epic: Sohrab and Rustum. mythical figure, about whom the action centers. To this type belongs *Sohrab and Rustum.* Arnold called his poem an "episode"; it is not a complete epic, but tells of one episode in the life of the great Persian hero, Rustum. At the same time, it evinces the epic form and spirit. The verse is dignified, the simile is freely employed, and the action centers

about the life of Rustum. Moreover, the poem mani-
fests the essential epic "objectivity" — the events of
the story speak for themselves without any personal re-
flections on the part of the author.

The terms "romance" and "tale" are somewhat loosely
employed. The former is used of a poem that is fabulous
or romantic in tone, as Spenser's *Faerie Queene*
Romance, or Scott's *Marmion*. The latter designates
and Tale. stories like many of Chaucer's *Canterbury
Tales*, or those contained in William Morris's *Earthly
Paradise*. Both forms are widely distributed in English
literature.

The tale is well represented by the third poem in this
book, *Enoch Arden*. This is primarily a story, and moves
definitely to a tragic conclusion. In the
Enoch Ar- opinion of some critics, the simplicity of the
den. narrative is unduly overlaid, by the elaborate
beauty of language and imagery. Yet the Tennyson
lover will be slow to admit that this emphasis on beauty
in any way detracts from the general effect, and *Enoch
Arden* will probably remain, among stories of English
country life in poetical form, the most representative and
popular. The reader would do well, in order to judge
the range of the tale in narrative poetry, to compare
Tennyson's poem with Chaucer's *Knightes Tale*, Longfellow's *The Bell of Atri*, and Masefield's *Right Royal*.

Two other forms may be included under the general
head of narrative poetry. The "idyl" ("idyll") is a
"little picture," usually with a pastoral setting.
Idyl, Didac- Examples are found in Milton's *L'Allegro* and
tic Poetry. *Il Penseroso*, and Burns's *The Cotter's Saturday
Night*. Tennyson's *Idylls of the King* are, of course,

familiar to all. Didactic poetry, wherein the aim is to teach a lesson or to draw a moral, is also frequently narrative in form. A well-known illustration is Goldsmith's *Deserted Village*.

Narrative poetry possesses features of peculiar interest and comprises a literary division of wide extent and great importance. The three poems which have been included in this book afford sound examples of its general forms and tendencies. A careful study of these poems will direct the mind towards a keener appreciation of all good poetry.

SAMUEL TAYLOR COLERIDGE

THE ANCIENT MARINER.

He stoppeth one of three.

THE RIME OF THE ANCIENT MARINER

IN SEVEN PARTS.

Argument.

How a ship having passed the Line was driven by storms to the cold
Country towards the South Pole; and how from thence she made her course
to the tropical Latitude of the Great Pacific Ocean; and of the strange things
that befell; and in what manner the Ancyent Marinere came back to his
own Country.

PART I

It is an ancient Mariner,
And he stoppeth one of three.
" By thy long gray beard and glittering eye,
Now wherefore stopp'st thou me?

An ancient Mariner meeteth three Gallants bidden to a wedding-feast and detaineth one.

" The Bridegroom's doors are opened wide,   5
And I am next of kin;
The guests are met, the feast is set:
May'st hear the merry din."

He holds him with his skinny hand,
" There was a ship," quoth he.   10
" Hold off! unhand me, gray-beard loon!"
Eftsoons his hand dropt he.

He holds him with his glittering eye —
The Wedding-Guest stood still,
And listens like a three years' child: 15
The Mariner hath his will.

The Wedding-Guest is spell-bound by the eye of the old seafaring man, and constrained to hear his tale.

1

The Wedding-Guest sat on a stone:
He cannot choose but hear;
And thus spake on that ancient man,
The bright-eyed Mariner.   20

"The ship was cheered, the harbor cleared,
Merrily did we drop
Below the kirk, below the hill,
Below the lighthouse top.

The Mariner tells how the ship sailed southward with a good wind and fair weather, till it reached the line.

"The sun came up upon the left,   25
Out of the sea came he!
And he shone bright, and on the right
Went down into the sea.

"Higher and higher every day,
Till over the mast at noon — "   30
The Wedding-Guest here beat his breast,
For he heard the loud bassoon.

The Wedding-Guest heareth the bridal music; but the Mariner continueth his tale.

The bride had paced into the hall,
Red as a rose is she;
Nodding their heads before her goes   35
The merry minstrelsy.

The Wedding-Guest he beat his breast,
Yet he cannot choose but hear;
And thus spake on that ancient man,
The bright-eyed Mariner.   40

The ship driven by a storm toward the south pole.

"And now the Storm-blast came, and he
Was tyrannous and strong:
He struck with his o'ertaking wings,
And chased us south along.

" With sloping masts and dripping prow,　　45
As who pursued with yell and blow
Still treads the shadow of his foe,
And forward bends his head,
The ship drove fast, loud roared the blast,
And southward aye we fled.　　50

" And now there came both mist and snow,
And it grew wondrous cold :
And ice, mast-high, came floating by,
As green as emerald.

" And through the drifts the snowy clifts　　55
Did send a dismal sheen :
Nor shapes of men nor beasts we ken —
The ice was all between.

The land of ice, and of fearful sounds where no living thing was to be seen.

" The ice was here, the ice was there,
The ice was all around :　　60
It cracked and growled, and roared and howled,
Like noises in a swound !

" At length did cross an Albatross,
Thorough the fog it came ;
As if it had been a Christian soul,　　65
We hailed it in God's name.

Till a great seabird, called the Albatross, came through the snow-fog, and was received with great joy and hospitality.

" It ate the food it ne'er had eat,
And round and round it flew.
The ice did split with a thunder-fit ;
The helmsman steered us through !　　70

And lo! the
Albatross
proved a
bird of good
omen, and
followeth the
ship as it
returned
northward
through fog
and floating
ice.

" And a good south wind sprung up behind;
The Albatross did follow,
And every day, for food or play,
Came to the Mariners' hollo!

" In mist or cloud, on mast or shroud,   75
It perched for vespers nine;
Whiles all the night, through fog-smoke white,
Glimmered the white moon-shine."

The ancient
Mariner in-
hospitably
killeth the
pious bird of
good omen.

" God save thee, ancient Mariner!
From the fiends, that plague thee thus! —   80
Why look'st thou so?"—" With my cross-bow
I shot the Albatross.

PART II.

" The Sun now rose upon the right;
Out of the sea came he,
Still hid in mist, and on the left   85
Went down into the sea.

" And the good south wind still blew behind,
But no sweet bird did follow,
Nor any day for food or play
Came to the mariners' hollo!   90

His shipmates
cry out against
the ancient
Mariner, for
killing the
bird of good
luck.

" And I had done a hellish thing,
And it would work 'em woe:
For all averred, I had killed the bird
That made the breeze to blow.
' Ah wretch!' said they, ' the bird to slay,   95
That made the breeze to blow!'

"And I had done a hellish thing."

"Instead of the cross, the Albatross
About my neck was hung."

"Nor dim nor red, like God's own head,
The glorious Sun uprist:
Then all averred, I had killed the bird
That brought the fog and mist.   100
'Twas right,' said they, 'such birds to slay,
That bring the fog and mist.'

But when the fog cleared off, they justify the same, and thus make themselves accomplices in the crime.

"The fair breeze blew, the white foam flew,
Tho furrow followed free ;
We were the first that ever burst   105
Into that silent sea.

The fair breeze continues; the ship enters the Pacific Ocean, and sails northward, even till it reaches the line.

"Down dropt the breeze, the sails dropt down,
'Twas sad as sad could be ;
And we did speak only to break
The silence of the sea !   110

The ship hath been suddenly becalmed.

"All in a hot and copper sky,
The bloody Sun, at noon,
Right up above the mast did stand,
No bigger than the Moon.

"Day after day, day after day,   115
We stuck, nor breath nor motion ;
As idle as a painted ship
Upon a painted ocean.

"Water, water, everywhere,
And all the boards did shrink ;   120
Water, water, everywhere
Nor any drop to drink.

And the Albatross begins to be avenged.

" The very deep did rot : O Christ !
That ever this should be !
Yea, slimy things did crawl with legs   125
Upon the slimy sea.

" About, about, in reel and rout
The death-fires danced at night ;
The water, like a witch's oils,
Burnt green, and blue, and white.   130

" And some in dreams assurèd were
Of the Spirit that plagued us so ;
Nine fathom deep he had followed us
From the land of mist and snow.

" And every tongue, through utter drought,   135
Was withered at the root ;
We could not speak, no more than if
We had been choked with soot.

" Ah ! well-a-day ! what evil looks
Had I from old and young !   140
Instead of the cross, the Albatross
About my neck was hung.

PART III.

" There passed a weary time.   Each throat
Was parched, and glazed each eye.
A weary time ! a weary time !   145
How glazed each weary eye,
When, looking westward, I beheld
A something in the sky.

A spirit had followed them; one of the invisible inhabitants of this planet, neither departed souls nor angels ; concerning whom the learned Jew, Josephus, and the Platonic Constantino-politan, Michael Psellus, may be consulted. They are very numerous, and there is no climate or element without one or more.

The ship-mates, in their sore distress would fain throw the whole guilt on the ancient Mariner : in sign whereof they hang the dead sea-bird round his neck.

The ancient Mariner be-holdeth a sign in the element afar off.

' At first it seemed a little speck,
And then it seemed a mist;   150
It moved and moved, and took at last
A certain shape, I wist.

"A speck, a mist, a shape, I wist!
And still it neared and neared:
As if it dodged a water-sprite,   155
It plunged and tacked and veered.

"With throats unslaked, with black lips baked,
We could nor laugh nor wail;
Through utter drought all dumb we stood!
I bit my arm, I sucked the blood,   160
And cried, ' A sail! a sail!'

At its nearer approach, it seemeth him to be a ship; and at a dear ransom he freeth his speech from the bonds of thirst.

"With throats unslaked, with black lips baked,
Agape they hear me call:
Gramercy! they for joy did grin,
And all at once their breath drew in,   165
As they were drinking all.

A flash of joy.

"' See! see!' (I cried) ' she tacks no more!
Hither to work us weal;
Without a breeze, without a tide,
She steadies with upright keel!'   170

And horror follows; for can it be a ship that comes onward without wind or tide?

"The western wave was all a-flame,
The day was well-nigh done!
Almost upon the western wave
Rested the broad bright Sun;
When that strange shape drove suddenly   175
Betwixt us and the Sun.

It seemeth him but the skeleton of a ship.

" And straight the Sun was flecked with bars,
(Heaven's Mother send us grace!)
As if through a dungeon-grate he peered
With broad and burning face.   180

" 'Alas!' (thought I, and my heart beat loud)
' How fast she nears and nears!
Are those her sails that glance in the sun,
Like restless gossameres?

And its ribs are seen as bars on the face of the setting Sun. The Spectre-Woman and her death-mate, and no other on board the skeleton ship. Like vessel, like crew!

" 'Are those her ribs through which the sun   185
Did peer, as through a grate?
And is that woman all her crew?
Is that a Death? and are there two?
Is Death that woman's mate?'

" Her lips were red, her looks were free,   190
Her locks were yellow as gold:
Her skin was as white as leprosy,
The Nightmare Life-in-Death was she,
Who thicks man's blood with cold.

Death and Life-in-Death have diced for the ship's crew, and she (the latter) winneth the ancient Mariner.

" The naked hulk alongside came,   195
And the twain were casting dice;
' The game is done! I've won! I've won!'
Quoth she, and whistles thrice.

No twilight within the courts of the Sun.

" The Sun's rim dips; the stars rush out;
At one stride comes the dark;   200
With far-heard whisper, o'er the sea,
Off shot the spectre-bark.

" We listened and looked sideways up !　　At the rising of the Moon,
Fear at my heart, as at a cup,
My life-blood seemed to sip !　205
The stars were dim, and thick the night,
The steersman's face by his lamp gleamed white,
From the sails the dew did drip —
Till clomb above the eastern bar
The hornèd Moon, with one bright star　210
Within the nether tip.

" One after one, by the star-dogged Moon,　one after another.
Too quick for groan or sigh,
Each turned his face with a ghastly pang,
And cursed me with his eye.　215

" Four times fifty living men,　his shipmates drop down dead.
(And I heard nor sigh nor groan)
With heavy thump, a lifeless lump,
They dropped down one by one.

" The souls did from their bodies fly, —　220　But Life-in-Death begins her work on the ancient Mariner.
They fled to bliss or woe !
And every soul, it passed me by,
Like the whizz of my cross-bow ! "

PART IV.

" I fear thee, ancient Mariner !　The Wedding-Guest feareth that a spirit is talking to him ; but the ancient
I fear thy skinny hand !　225
And thou art long, and lank, and brown,
As is the ribbed sea-sand.

" I fear thee and thy glittering eye,
And thy skinny hand, so brown." —

Mariner as-
sureth him of
his bodily life,
and pro-
ceedeth to
relate his
horrible pen-
ance.

" Fear not, fear not, thou Wedding-Guest !　230
This body dropt not down.

" Alone, alone, all, all alone,
Alone on a wide, wide sea !
And never a saint took pity on
My soul in agony.　　　　　　　235

He despiseth
the creatures
of the calm,

" The many men, so beautiful !
And they all dead did lie :
And a thousand thousand slimy things
Lived on ; and so did I.

and envieth
that they
should live,
and so many
lie dead.

" I looked upon the rotting sea,　240
And drew my eyes away ;
I looked upon the rotting deck,
And there the dead men lay.

" I looked to heaven, and tried to pray ;
But or ever a prayer had gusht,　245
A wicked whisper came, and made
My heart as dry as dust.

" I closed my lids, and kept them close,
And the balls like pulses beat ;
For the sky and the sea, and the sea and the sky,
Lay like a load on my weary eye,　251
And the dead were at my feet.

But the curse
liveth for him
in the eye of
the dead men.

" The cold sweat melted from their limbs,
Nor rot nor reek did they :
The look with which they looked on me　255
Had never passed away.

"An orphan's curse would drag to hell,
A spirit from on high;
But oh! more horrible than that
Is a curse in a dead man's eye!　　260
Seven days, seven nights, I saw that curse,
And yet I could not die.

"The moving Moon went up the sky,
And nowhere did abide:
Softly she was going up,　　265
And a star or two beside—

In his loneliness and fixedness he yearneth towards the journeying Moon, and the stars that still sojourn, yet still move onward; and everywhere the blue sky belongs to them, and is their appointed rest, and their native country and their own natural homes, which they enter unannounced, as lords that are certainly expected and yet there is a silent joy at their arrival.

"Her beams bemocked the sultry main,
Like April hoar-frost spread;
But where the ship's huge shadow lay,
The charmèd water burnt alway　　270
A still and awful red.

"Beyond the shadow of the ship,
I watched the water-snakes:
They moved in tracks of shining white,
And when they reared, the elfish light　　275
Fell off in hoary flakes.

By the light of the Moon he beholdeth God's creatures of the great calm.

"Within the shadow of the ship
I watched their rich attire:
Blue, glossy green, and velvet black,
They coiled and swam; and every track　　280
Was a flash of golden fire.

"O happy living things! no tongue
Their beauty might declare:

Their beauty and their happiness.

He blesseth
them in his
heart.

A spring of love gushed from my heart,
And I blessed them unaware :   285
Sure my kind saint took pity on me,
And I blessed them unaware.

The spell be-
gins to break.

" The selfsame moment I could pray ;
And from my neck so free
The Albatross fell off, and sank   290
Like lead into the sea.

PART V.

" Oh sleep ! it is a gentle thing,
Beloved from pole to pole !
To Mary Queen the praise be given !
She sent the gentle sleep from heaven,   295
That slid into my soul.

By grace of the
holy Mother,
the ancient
Mariner is re-
freshed with
rain.

" The silly buckets on the deck,
That had so long remained,
I dreamt that they were filled with dew
And when I awoke, it rained.   300

" My lips were wet, my throat was cold,
My garments all were dank ;
Sure I had drunken in my dreams,
And still my body drank.

" I moved, and could not feel my limbs :   305
I was so light — almost
I thought that I had died in sleep,
And was a blessèd ghost.

"The Albatross fell off, and sank
Like lead into the sea."

" And soon I heard a roaring wind :
It did not come anear ;　　　　　　　　　310
But with its sound it shook the sails,
That were so thin and sere.

" The upper air burst into life !
And a hundred fire-flags sheen,
To and fro they were hurried about !　　315
And to and fro, and in and out,
The wan stars danced between.

" And the coming wind did roar more loud,
And the sails did sigh like sedge ;
And the rain poured down from one black cloud ;
The Moon was at its edge.　　　　　　321

" The thick black cloud was cleft, and still
The Moon was at its side :
Like waters shot from some high crag,
The lightning fell with never a jag,　　325
A river steep and wide.

" The loud wind never reached the ship,
Yet now the ship moved on !
Beneath the lightning and the Moon
The dead men gave a groan.　　　　　330

" They groaned, they stirred, they all uprose,
Nor spake, nor moved their eyes ;
It had been strange, even in a dream,
To have seen those dead men rise.

" The helmsman steered, the ship moved on ; 335
Yet never a breeze up blew ;

He heareth sounds and seeth strange sights and commotions in the sky and the element.

The bodies of the ship's crew are inspirited, and the ship moves on ;

The mariners all 'gan work the ropes,
Where they were wont to do ;
They raised their limbs like lifeless tools —
We were a ghastly crew.   340

" The body of my brother's son
Stood by me, knee to knee :
The body and I pulled at one rope
But he said nought to me. — "

" I fear thee, ancient Mariner ! "   345
" Be calm, thou Wedding-Guest !
'Twas not those souls that fled in pain,
Which to their corses came again,
But a troop of spirits blest :

" For when it dawned — they dropped their arms,
And clustered round the mast ;   351
Sweet sounds rose slowly through their mouths,
And from their bodies passed.

" Around, around, flew each sweet sound,
Then darted to the Sun ;   355
Slowly the sounds came back again,
Now mixed, now one by one.

" Sometimes a-dropping from the sky
I heard the sky-lark sing ;
Sometimes all the little birds that are,   360
How they seemed to fill the sea and air
With their sweet jargoning !

" And now 'twas like all instruments,
Now like a lonely flute ;
And now it is an angel's song,   365
That makes the heavens be mute.

" It ceased ; yet still the sails made on
A pleasant noise till noon,
A noise like of a hidden brook
In the leafy month of June,   370
That to the sleeping woods all night
Singeth a quiet tune.

" Till noon we quietly sailed on,
Yet never a breeze did breathe :
Slowly and smoothly went the ship,   375
Moved onward from beneath.

" Under the keel nine fathom deep,
From the land of mist and snow,
The spirit slid ; and it was he
That made the ship to go.   380
The sails at noon left off their tune,
And the ship stood still also.

The lonesome Spirit from the south pole carries on the ship as far as the line, in obedience to the angelic troop, but still requireth vengeance.

" The Sun, right up above the mast,
Had fixed her to the ocean ;
But in a minute she 'gan stir,   385
With a short uneasy motion —
Backwards and forwards half her length,
With a short uneasy motion.

" Then, like a pawing horse let go,
She made a sudden bound :   390

It flung the blood into my head,
And I fell down in a swound.

The Polar
Spirit's fellow-
dæmons, the
invisible in-
habitants of
the element,
take part in
his wrong; and
two of them
relate, one to
the other, that
penance long
and heavy
for the ancient
Mariner hath
been accorded
to the Polar
Spirit, who
returneth
southward.

" How long in that same fit I lay,
I have not to declare ;
But ere my living life returned,   395
I heard, and in my soul discerned,
Two voices in the air.

" ' Is it he ? ' quoth one, ' Is this the man ?
By Him who died on cross,
With his cruel bow he laid full low   400
The harmless Albatross.

" ' The spirit who bideth by himself
In the land of mist and snow,
He loved the bird that loved the man
Who shot him with his bow.'   405

" The other was a softer voice,
As soft as honey-dew :
Quoth he, ' The man hath penance done,
And penance more will do.'

PART VI.

First Voice.

" ' But tell me, tell me ! speak again,   410
Thy soft response renewing —
What makes that ship drive on so fast ?
What is the ocean doing ? '

Second Voice.

" ' Still as a slave before his lord,
The ocean hath no blast ;   415
His great bright eye most silently
Up to the Moon is cast —

" ' If he may know which way to go ;
For she guides him smooth or grim.
See, brother, see ! how graciously   420
She looketh down on him.'

First Voice.

" ' But why drives on that ship so fast,
Without or wave or wind ? '

The Mariner hath been cast into a trance ; for the angelic power causeth the vessel to drive northward faster than human life could endure.

Second Voice.

' The air is cut away before,
And closes from behind.   425

" ' Fly, brother, fly ! more high, more high !
Or we shall be belated :
For slow and slow that ship will go,
When the Mariner's trance is abated.'

" I woke, and we were sailing on   430
As in a gentle weather :
'Twas night, calm night, the Moon was high ;
The dead men stood together.

The supernatural motion is retarded ; the Mariner awakes, and his penance begins anew.

" All stood together on the deck,
For a charnel-dungeon fitter :   435
All fixed on me their stony eyes,
That in the Moon did glitter.

"The pang, the curse, with which they died,
Had never passed away:
I could not draw my eyes from theirs,   440
Nor turn them up to pray.

The curse is
finally ex-
piated.
"And now this spell was snapt: once more
I viewed the ocean green,
And looked far forth, yet little saw
Of what had else been seen —   445

"Like one, that on a lonesome road
Doth walk in fear and dread,
And having once turned round walks on,
And turns no more his head;
Because he knows, a frightful fiend   450
Doth close behind him tread.

"But soon there breathed a wind on me
Nor sound nor motion made:
Its path was not upon the sea,
In ripple or in shade.   455

"It raised my hair, it fanned my cheek
Like a meadow-gale of spring —
It mingled strangely with my fears,
Yet it felt like a welcoming.

"Swiftly, swiftly flew the ship,   460
Yet she sailed softly too:
Sweetly, sweetly blew the breeze —
On me alone it blew.

"Oh! dream of joy! is this indeed
The lighthouse top I see?   465
Is this the hill? is this the kirk?
Is this mine own countree?

And the ancient Mariner beholdeth his native country.

" We drifted o'er the harbor-bar,
And I with sobs did pray —
' O let me be awake, my God!   470
Or let me sleep alway.'

" The harbor-bay was clear as glass,
So smoothly it was strewn!
And on the bay the moonlight lay,
And the shadow of the Moon.   475

" The rock shone bright, the kirk no less,
That stands above the rock:
The moonlight steeped in silentness
The steady weathercock.

" And the bay was white with silent light,   480
Till, rising from the same,
Full many shapes, that shadows were,
In crimson colors came.

The angelic spirits leave the dead bodies,

" A little distance from the prow
Those crimson shadows were: 485
I turned my eyes upon the deck —
Oh Christ! what saw I there!

and appear in their own forms of light.

" Each corse lay flat, lifeless and flat,
And, by the holy rood!
A man all light, a seraph-man,   490
On every corse there stood.

"This seraph-band, each waved his hand;
It was a heavenly sight!
They stood as signals to the land,
Each one a lovely light;   495

"This seraph-band, each waved his hand:
No voice did they impart —
No voice; but oh! the silence sank
Like music on my heart.

"But soon I heard the dash of oars;   500
I heard the Pilot's cheer;
My head was turned perforce away,
And I saw a boat appear.

"The Pilot and the Pilot's boy,
I heard them coming fast: 505
Dear Lord in Heaven! it was a joy
The dead men could not blast.

"I saw a third — I heard his voice:
It is the Hermit good!
He singeth loud his godly hymns   510
That he makes in the wood.
He'll shrieve my soul, he'll wash away
The Albatross's blood.

PART VII.

The Hermit of
the wood

"This Hermit good lives in that wood
Which slopes down to the sea.   515
How loudly his sweet voice he rears!
He loves to talk with marineres
That come from a far countree.

" He kneels at morn, and noon, and eve —
He hath a cushion plump :　　　　　520
It is the moss that wholly hides
The rotted old oak-stump.

" The skiff-boat neared : I heard them talk
' Why, this is strange, I trow !
Where are those lights so many and fair,　525
That signal made but now ?'

" ' Strange, by my faith !' the Hermit said —
' And they answered not our cheer !
The planks look warped ! and see those sails,
How thin they are and sere !　　　530
I never saw aught like to them,
Unless perchance it were

approacheth
the ship with
wonder.

" ' Brown skeletons of leaves that lag
My forest-brook along ;
When the ivy-tod is heavy with snow,　535
And the owlet whoops to the wolf below,
That eats the she-wolf's young.'

" ' Dear Lord ! it hath a fiendish look — '
(The Pilot made reply)
' I am a-feared ' — ' Push on, push on !'　540
Said the Hermit cheerily.

" The boat came closer to the ship,
But I nor spake nor stirred ;
The boat came close beneath the ship,
And straight a sound was heard.　　545

The ship sud-
denly sinketh.
" Under the water it rumbled on,
    Still louder and more dread :
It reached the ship, it split the bay ;
    The ship went down like lead.

The ancient
Mariner is
saved in the
Pilot's boat.
" Stunned by that loud and dreadful sound,   550
    Which sky and ocean smote,
Like one that hath been seven days drowned
    My body lay afloat;
But, swift as dreams, myself I found
    Within the Pilot's boat.   555

" Upon the whirl, where sank the ship,
    The boat spun round and round ;
And all was still, save that the hill
    Was telling of the sound.

" I moved my lips — the Pilot shrieked   56b
    And fell down in a fit;
The holy Hermit raised his eyes,
    And prayed where he did sit.

" I took the oars : the Pilot's boy,
    Who now doth crazy go,   565
Laughed loud and long, and all the while
    His eyes went to and fro.
' Ha ! ha !' quoth he, ' full plain I see,
    The Devil knows how to row.'

" And now, all in my own countree,   57c
    I stood on the firm land !
The Hermit stepped forth from the boat,
    And scarcely he could stand

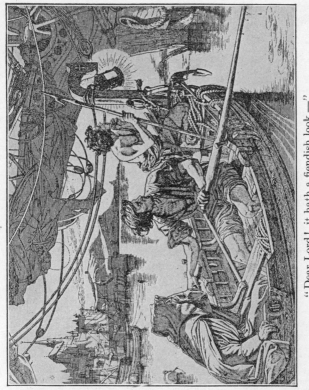

"Dear Lord! it hath a fiendish look —"

"O shrieve me, shrieve me, holy man!"

" ' O shrieve me, shrieve me, holy man !'
The Hermit crossed his brow.   575
' Say quick,' quoth he, ' I bid thee say —
What manner of man art thou ? '

" Forthwith this frame of mine was wrenched
With a woful agony,
Which forced me to begin my tale ;   580
And then it left me free.

" Since then, at an uncertain hour,
That agony returns ;
And till my ghastly tale is told,
This heart within me burns.   585

" I pass, like night, from land to land ;
I have strange power of speech ;
That moment that his face I see,
I know the man that must hear me :
To him my tale I teach.   590

" What loud uproar bursts from that door !
The wedding-guests are there :
But in the garden-bower the bride
And bride-maids singing are :
And hark the little vesper bell,   595
Which biddeth me to prayer !

" O Wedding-Guest ! this soul hath been
Alone on a wide, wide sea :
So lonely 'twas, that God himself
Scarce seemèd there to be.   600

"O sweeter than the marriage-feast,
'Tis sweeter far to me,
To walk together to the kirk
With a goodly company! —

"To walk together to the kirk,   605
And all together pray,
While each to his great Father bends,
Old men, and babes, and loving friends,
And youths and maidens gay!

and to teach,
by his own ex-
ample, love
and reverence
to all things
that God
made and
loveth.

"Farewell, farewell! but this I tell   610
To thee, thou Wedding-Guest!
He prayeth well, who loveth well
Both man and bird and beast.

"He prayeth best, who loveth best
All things both great and small;   615
For the dear God who loveth us,
He made and loveth all."

The Mariner, whose eye is bright,
Whose beard with age is hoar,
Is gone: and now the Wedding-Guest   620
Turned from the bridegroom's door.

He went like one that hath been stunned,
And is of sense forlorn:
A sadder and a wiser man
He rose the morrow morn.   625

MATTHEW ARNOLD

SOHRAB AND RUSTUM.

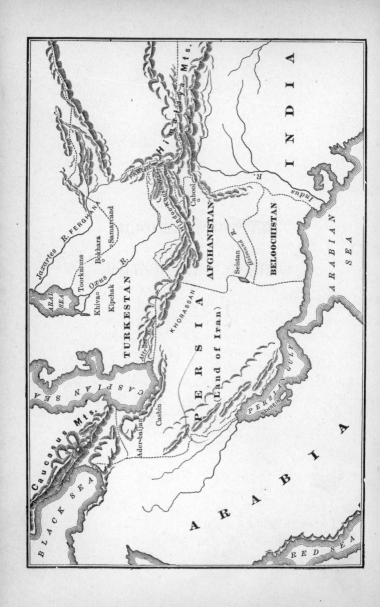

SOHRAB AND RUSTUM

AN EPISODE.

—◦—

AND the first gray of morning filled the east,
And the fog rose out of the Oxus stream.
But all the Tartar camp along the stream
Was hushed, and still the men were plunged in sleep.
Sohrab alone, he slept not; all night long   5
He had lain wakeful, tossing on his bed:
But when the gray dawn stole into his tent,
He rose, and clad himself, and girt his sword,
And took his horseman's cloak, and left his tent,
And went abroad into the cold wet fog,   10
Through the dim camp to Peran-Wisa's tent.

   Through the black Tartar tents he passed, which stood
Clustering like bee-hives on the low flat strand   *Simile*
Of Oxus, where the summer-floods o'erflow
When the sun melts the snows in high Pamere;   15
Through the black tents he passed, o'er that low strand,
And to a hillock came, a little back
From the stream's brink, — the spot where first a boat,
Crossing the stream in summer, scrapes the land.
The men of former times had crowned the top   20
With a clay fort; but that was fallen, and now
The Tartars built there Peran-Wisa's tent,
A dome of laths, and o'er it felts were spread.

And Sohrab came there, and went in, and stood
Upon the thick piled carpets in the tent,   25
And found the old man sleeping on his bed
Of rugs and felts, and near him lay his arms.
And Peran-Wisa heard him, though the step
Was dulled; for he slept light, an old man's sleep;
And he rose quickly on one arm, and said,—   30
  " Who art thou? for it is not yet clear dawn.
Speak! is there news, or any night alarm? "
  But Sohrab came to the bedside, and said,—
" Thou know'st me, Peran-Wisa! it is I.
The sun has not yet risen, and the foe   35
Sleep: but I sleep not; all night long I lie
Tossing and wakeful, and I come to thee.
For so did King Afrasiab bid me seek
Thy counsel, and to heed thee as thy son,
In Samarcand, before the army marched;   40
And I will tell thee what my heart desires.
Thou know'st if, since from Ader-baijan first
I came among the Tartars, and bore arms,
I have still served Afrasiab well, and shown,
At my boy's years, the courage of a man.   45
This too thou know'st, that while I still bear on
The conquering Tartar ensigns through the world,
And beat the Persians back on every field,
I seek one man, one man, and one alone,—
Rustum, my father; who I hoped should greet,   50
Should one day greet, upon some well-fought field,
His not unworthy, not inglorious son.
So I long hoped, but him I never find.
Come then, hear now, and grant me what I ask.
Let the two armies rest to-day; but I   55
Will challenge forth the bravest Persian lords

"I came among the Tartars and bore arms."
TARTAR CHIEFTAINS.

To meet me, man to man : if I prevail,
Rustum will surely hear it ; if I fall —
Old man, the dead need no one, claim no kin.
Dim is the rumor of a common fight   60
Where host meets host, and many names are sunk ;
But of a single combat fame speaks clear."
   He spoke ; and Peran-Wisa took the hand
Of the young man in his, and sighed, and said, —
   " O Sohrab, an unquiet heart is thine !   65
Canst thou not rest among the Tartar chiefs,
And share the battle's common chance with us
Who love thee, but must press forever first,
In single fight incurring single risk,
To find a father thou hast never seen ?   70
That were far best, my son, to stay with us
Unmurmuring ; in our tents, while it is war,
And when 'tis truce, then in Afrasiab's towns.
But if this one desire indeed rules all,
To seek out Rustum — seek him not through fight !   75
Seek him in peace, and carry to his arms,
O Sohrab, carry an unwounded son !
But far hence seek him, for he is not here.
For now it is not as when I was young,
When Rustum was in front of every fray :   80
But now he keeps apart, and sits at home,
In Seistan, with Zal, his father old ;
Whether that his own mighty strength at last
Feels the abhorred approaches of old age ;
Or in some quarrel with the Persian king.   85
There go ! — Thou wilt not ?   Yet my heart forebodes
Danger or death awaits thee on this field.
Fain would I know thee safe and well, though lost
To us ; fain therefore send thee hence in peace

To seek thy father, not seek single fights   90
In vain.   But who can keep the lion's cub
From ravening, and who govern Rustum's son?
Go: I will grant thee what thy heart desires."
   So said he, and dropped Sohrab's hand, and left
His bed, and the warm rugs whereon he lay;   95
And o'er his chilly limbs his woollen coat
He passed, and tied his sandals on his feet,
And threw a white cloak round him, and he took
In his right hand a ruler's staff, no sword;
And on his head he set his sheep-skin cap,   100
Black, glossy, curled, the fleece of Kara-Kul;
And raised the curtain of his tent, and called
His herald to his side, and went abroad.
   The sun by this had risen, and cleared the fog
From the broad Oxus and the glittering sands.   105
And from their tents the Tartar horseman filed
Into the open plain: so Haman bade, —
Haman, who next to Peran-Wisa ruled
The host, and still was in his lusty prime.
From their black tents, long files of horse, they streamed;
As when some gray November morn the files,   111
In marching order spread, of long-necked cranes
Stream over Casbin and the southern slopes
Of Elburz, from the Aralian estuaries,
Or some frore Caspian reed-bed, southward bound   115
For the warm Persian seaboard, — so they streamed.
The Tartars of the Oxus, the king's guard,
First, with black sheep-skin caps and with long spears;
Large men, large steeds, who from Bokhara came
And Khiva, and ferment the milk of mares.   120
Next, the more temperate Toorkmuns of the south,
The Tukas, and the lances of Salore,

And those from Attruck and the Caspian sands;
Light men on light steeds, who only drink
The acrid milk of camels, and their wells.   125
And then a swarm of wandering horse, who came
From far, and a more doubtful service owned, —
The Tartars of Ferghana, from the banks
Of the Jaxartes, men with scanty beards
And close-set skull-caps; and those wilder hordes   130
Who roam o'er Kipchak and the northern waste,
Kalmucks and unkempt Kuzzaks, tribes who stray
Nearest the pole, and wandering Kirghizzes,
Who come on shaggy ponies from Pamere, —
These all filed out from camp into the plain.   135
And on the other side the Persians formed, —
First a light cloud of horse, Tartars they seemed,
The Ilyats of Khorassan; and behind,
The royal troops of Persia, horse and foot,
Marshalled battalions bright in burnished steel.   140
But Peran-Wisa with his herald came,
Threading the Tartar squadrons to the front,
And with his staff kept back the foremost ranks.
And when Ferood, who led the Persians, saw
That Peran-Wisa kept the Tartars back,   145
He took his spear, and to the front he came,
And checked his ranks, and fixed them where they stood.
And the old Tartar came upon the sand
Betwixt the silent hosts, and spake, and said, —
   "Ferood, and ye, Persians and Tartars, hear!   150
Let there be truce between the hosts to-day.
But choose a champion from the Persian lords
To fight our champion Sohrab, man to man."
   As in the country, on a morn in June,
When the dew glistens on the pearled ears,   155

A shiver runs through the deep corn for joy, —
So, when they heard what Peran-Wisa said,
A thrill through all the Tartar squadrons ran
Of pride and hope for Sohrab, whom they loved.

But as a troop of pedlars from Cabool   160
Cross underneath the Indian Caucasus,
That vast sky-neighboring mountain of milk snow :
Crossing so high, that, as they mount, they pass
Long flocks of travelling birds dead on the snow,
Choked by the air, and scarce can they themselves   165
Slake their parched throats with sugared mulberries ;
In single file they move, and stop their breath,
For fear they should dislodge the o'erhanging snows, —
So the pale Persians held their breath with fear.

And to Ferood his brother chiefs came up   170
To counsel ; Gudurz and Zoarrah came,
And Feraburz, who ruled the Persian host
Second, and was the uncle of the king ;
These came and counselled, and then Gudurz said, —

"Ferood, shame bids us take their challenge up,   175
Yet champion have we none to match this youth.
He has the wild stag's foot, the lion's heart.
But Rustum came last night ; aloof he sits
And sullen, and has pitched his tents apart.
Him will I seek, and carry to his ear   180
The Tartar challenge, and this young man's name ;
Haply he will forget his wrath, and fight.
Stand forth the while, and take their challenge up."

So spake he ; and Ferood stood forth and cried, —
"Old man, be it agreed as thou hast said !   185
Let Sohrab arm, and we will find a man."

He spake ; and Peran-Wisa turned, and strode
Back through the opening squadrons to his tent.

Held a falcon on his wrist.

TURCOMAN FALCONERS.

But through the anxious Persians Gudurz ran,
And crossed the camp which lay behind, and reached,   190
Out on the sands beyond it, Rustum's tents.
Of scarlet cloth they were, and glittering gay,
Just pitched ; the high pavilion in the midst
Was Rustum's, and his men lay camped around.
And Gudurz entered Rustum's tent, and found   195
Rustum ; his morning meal was done, but still
The table stood before him, charged with food, —
A side of roasted sheep, and cakes of bread,
And dark-green melons ; and there Rustum sate
Listless, and held a falcon on his wrist,   200
And played with it ; but Gudurz came and stood
Before him ; and he looked, and saw him stand,
And with a cry sprang up, and dropped the bird,
And greeted Gudurz with both hands, and said, —
 "Welcome ! these eyes could see no better sight.   205
What news ? but sit down first, and eat and drink."
 But Gudurz stood in the tent-door, and said, —
"Not now.   A time will come to eat and drink,
But not to-day : to-day has other needs.
The armies are drawn out, and stand at gaze ;   210
For, from the Tartars is a challenge brought
To pick a champion from the Persian lords
To fight their champion — and thou know'st his name :
Sohrab men call him, but his birth is hid.
O Rustum, like thy might is this young man's !   215
He has the wild stag's foot, the lion's heart ;
And he is young, and Iran's chiefs are old,
Or else too weak ; and all eyes turn to thee.
Come down and help us, Rustum, or we lose ! "
 He spoke ; but Rustum answered with a smile, —   220
" Go to ! if Iran's chiefs are old, then I

Am older.   If the young are weak, the king
Errs strangely ; for the king, for Kai Khosroo,
Himself is young, and honors younger men,
And lets the aged moulder to their graves.   225
Rustum he loves no more, but loves the young :
The young may rise at Sohrab's vaunts, not I.
For what care I, though all speak Sohrab's fame ?
For would that I myself had such a son,
And not that one slight helpless girl I have !   230
A son so famed, so brave, to send to war,
And I to tarry with the snow-haired Zal,
My father, whom the robber Afghans vex,
And clip his borders short, and drive his herds,
And he has none to guard his weak old age.   235
There would I go, and hang my armor up,
And with my great name fence that weak old man,
And spend the goodly treasures I have got,
And rest my age, and hear of Sohrab's fame,
And leave to death the hosts of thankless kings,   240
And with these slaughterous hands draw sword no more."

    He spoke, and smiled ; and Gudurz made reply, —
" What then, O Rustum, will men say to this,
When Sohrab dares our bravest forth, and seeks
Thee most of all, and thou, whom he most seeks,   245
Hidest thy face ?   Take heed lest men should say, —
Like some old miser, Rustum hoards his fame,
And shuns to peril it with younger men."
And, greatly moved, then Rustum made reply, —
" O Gudurz, wherefore dost thou say such words ?   250
Thou knowest better words than this to say.
What is one more, one less, obscure or famed,
Valiant or craven, young or old, to me ?
Are not they mortal ? am not I myself ?

But who for men of naught would do great deeds ?   255
Come, thou shalt see how Rustum hoards his fame !
But I will fight unknown, and in plain arms :
Let not men say of Rustum, he was matched
In single fight with any mortal man."
  He spoke, and frowned ; and Gudurz turned, and ran   260
Back quickly through the camp in fear and joy, —
Fear at his wrath, but joy that Rustum came.
But Rustum strode to his tent-door, and called
His followers in, and bade them bring his arms,
And clad himself in steel.   The arms he chose   265
Were plain, and on his shield was no device ;
Only his helm was rich, inlaid with gold,
And, from the fluted spine a-top, a plume
Of horse-hair waved, a scarlet horse-hair plume.
So armed, he issued forth ; and Ruksh, his horse,   270
Followed him like a faithful hound at heel, —
Ruksh, whose renown was noised through all the earth,
The horse whom Rustum on a foray once
Did in Bokhara by the river find
A colt beneath its dam, and drove him home,   275
And reared him ; a bright bay, with lofty crest,
Dight with a saddle-cloth of broidered green
Crusted with gold, and on the ground were worked
All beasts of chase, all beasts which hunters know.
So followed, Rustum left his tents, and crossed   280
The camp, and to the Persian host appeared.
And all the Persians knew him, and with shouts
Hailed ; but the Tartars knew not who he was.
And dear as the wet diver to the eyes
Of his pale wife who waits and weeps on shore,   285
By sandy Bahrein, in the Persian Gulf,
Plunging all day in the blue waves, at night,

Having made up his tale of precious pearls
Rejoins her in their hut upon the sands, —
So dear to the pale Persians Rustum came.   290
    And Rustum to the Persian front advanced ;
And Sohrab armed in Haman's tent, and came.
And as a-field the reapers cut a swath
Down through the middle of a rich man's corn,
And on each side are squares of standing corn,   295
And in the midst a stubble short and bare, —
So on each side were squares of men, with spears
Bristling, and in the midst the open sand.
And Rustum came upon the sand, and cast
His eyes toward the Tartar tents, and saw   300
Sohrab come forth, and eyed him as he came.
    As some rich woman, on a winter's morn,
Eyes through her silken curtains the poor drudge
Who with numb blackened fingers makes her fire, —
At cock-crow, on a starlit winter's morn,   305
When the frost flowers the whitened window-panes, —
And wonders how she lives, and what the thoughts
Of that poor drudge may be ; so Rustum eyed
The unknown adventurous youth, who from afar
Came seeking Rustum, and defying forth   310
All the most valiant chiefs ; long he perused
His spirited air, and wondered who he was.
For very young he seemed, tenderly reared ;
Like some young cypress, tall and dark and straight,
Which in a queen's secluded garden throws   315
Its slight dark shadow on a moonlit turf,
By midnight, to a bubbling fountain's sound, —
So slender Sohrab seemed, so softly reared.
And a deep pity entered Rustum's soul
As he beheld him coming ; and he stood,   320

And beckoned to him with his hand ; and said, —
  " O thou young man, the air of heaven is soft,
And warm, and pleasant ; but the grave is cold !
Heaven's air is better than the cold dead grave.
Behold me !   I am vast, and clad in iron,   325
And tried ; and I have stood on many a field
Of blood, and I have fought with many a foe :
Never was that field lost, or that foe saved.
O Sohrab, wherefore wilt thou rush on death ?
Be governed : quit the Tartar host, and come   330
To Iran, and be as my son to me,
And fight beneath my banner till I die !
There are no youths in Iran brave as thou."
  So he spake, mildly.   Sohrab heard his voice,
The mighty voice of Rustum, and he saw   335
His giant figure planted on the sand,
Sole, like some single tower, which a chief
Hath builded on the waste in former years
Against the robbers ; and he saw that head,
Streaked with its first gray hairs ; hope filled his soul,   340
And he ran forward, and embraced his knees,
And clasped his hand within his own, and said, —
  " Oh, by thy father's head ! by thine own soul !
Art thou not Rustum ?   Speak ! art thou not he ? "
  But Rustum eyed askance the kneeling youth,   345
And turned away, and spake to his own soul, —
  " Ah me !   I muse what this young fox may mean !
False, wily, boastful, are these Tartar boys.
For if I now confess this thing he asks,
And hide it not, but say, *Rustum is here* !   350
He will not yield indeed, nor quit our foes ;
But he will find some pretext not to fight,
And praise my fame, and proffer courteous gifts,

A belt or sword perhaps, and go his way.
And on a feast-tide, in Afrasiab's hall   355
In Samarcand, he will arise and cry, —
   ' I challenged once, when the two armies camped
Beside the Oxus, all the Persian lords
To cope with me in single fight; but they
Shrank, only Rustum dared; then he and I   360
Changed gifts, and went on equal terms away.'
So will he speak, perhaps, while men applaud;
Then were the chiefs of Iran shamed through me."
   And then he turned, and sternly spake aloud, —
" Rise! wherefore dost thou vainly question thus   365
Of Rustum?   I am here, whom thou hast called
By challenge forth; make good thy vaunt, or yield!
Is it with Rustum only thou wouldst fight?
Rash boy, men look on Rustum's face, and flee!
For well I know, that did great Rustum stand   370
Before thy face this day, and were revealed,
There would be then no talk of fighting more.
But being what I am, I tell thee this, —
Do thou record it in thine inmost soul:
Either thou shalt renounce thy vaunt, and yield,   375
Or else thy bones shall strew this sand, till winds
Bleach them, or Oxus with his summer-floods,
Oxus in summer wash them all away."
   He spoke; and Sohrab answered, on his feet, —
" Art thou so fierce?   Thou wilt not fright me so!   380
I am no girl, to be made pale by words.
Yet this thou hast said well, did Rustum stand
Here on this field, there were no fighting then.
But Rustum is far hence, and we stand here.
Begin! thou art more vast, more dread than I;   385
And thou art proved, I know, and I am young

But yet success sways with the breath of Heaven.
And though thou thinkest that thou knowest sure
Thy victory, yet thou canst not surely know.
For we are all, like swimmers in the sea,   390
Poised on the top of a huge wave of fate,
Which hangs uncertain to which side to fall;
And whether it will heave us up to land,
Or whether it will roll us out to sea, —
Back out to sea, to the deep waves of death, —   395
We know not, and no search will make us know:
Only the event will teach us in its hour."

    He spoke; and Rustum answered not, but hurled
His spear: down from the shoulder, down it came,
As on some partridge in the corn a hawk,   400
That long has towered in the airy clouds,
Drops like a plummet; Sohrab saw it come,
And sprang aside, quick as a flash; the spear
Hissed, and went quivering down into the sand,
Which it sent flying wide.   Then Sohrab threw   405
In turn, and full struck Rustum's shield; sharp rang
The iron plates rang sharp, but turned the spear.
And Rustum seized his club, which none but he
Could wield; an unlopped trunk it was, and huge,
Still rough, — like those which men in treeless plains   410
To build them boats fish from the flooded rivers,
Hyphasis or Hydaspes, when, high up
By their dark springs, the wind in winter-time
Hath made in Himalayan forests wrack,
And strewn the channels with torn boughs, — so huge   415
The club which Rustum lifted now, and struck
One stroke; but again Sohrab sprang aside,
Lithe as the glancing snake, and the club came
Thundering to earth, and leapt from Rustum's hand.

And Rustum followed his own blow, and fell   420
To his knees, and with his fingers clutched the sand.
And now might Sohrab have unsheathed his sword,
And pierced the mighty Rustum while he lay
Dizzy, and on his knees, and choked with sand ;
But he looked on, and smiled, nor bared his sword,   425
But courteously drew back, and spoke, and said, —
   " Thou strik'st too hard ! that club of thine will float
Upon the summer-floods, and not my bones.
But rise, and be not wroth ! not wroth am I ;
No, when I see thee, wrath forsakes my soul.   430
Thou say'st thou art not Rustum ; be it so !
Who art thou, then, that canst so touch my soul?
Boy as I am, I have seen battles too, —
Have waded foremost in their bloody waves,
And heard their hollow roar of dying men ;   435
But never was my heart thus touched before.
Are they from Heaven, these softenings of the heart?
O thou old warrior, let us yield to Heaven !
Come, plant we here in earth our angry spears,
And make a truce, and sit upon this sand,   440
And pledge each other in red wine, like friends,
And thou shall talk to me of Rustum's deeds.
There are enough foes in the Persian host,
Whom I may meet, and strike, and feel no pang ;
Champions enough Afrasiab has, whom thou   445
May'st fight ; fight *them*, when they confront thy spear !
But oh, let there be peace 'twixt thee and me ! "
   He ceased ; but while he spake, Rustum had risen,
And stood erect, trembling with rage ; his club
He left to lie, but had regained his spear,   450
Whose fiery point now in his mailed right hand
Blazed bright and baleful, like that autumn-star,

The baleful sign of fevers; dust had soiled
His stately crest, and dimmed his glittering arms.
His breast heaved, his lips foamed, and twice his voice   455
Was choked with rage; at last these words broke way : —
    " Girl ! nimble with thy feet, not with thy hands !
Curled minion, dancer, coiner of sweet words !
Fight, let me hear thy hateful voice no more !
Thou art not in Afrasiab's garden now   460
With Tartar girls, with whom thou art wont to dance;
But on the Oxus-sands, and in the dance
Of battle, and with me, who make no play
Of war: I fight it out, and hand to hand.
Speak not to me of truce, and pledge, and wine !   465
Remember all thy valor; try thy feints
And cunning! all the pity I had is gone,
Because thou hast shamed me before both the hosts
With thy light skipping tricks and thy girl's wiles."
    He spoke; and Sohrab kindled at his taunts,   470
And he too drew his sword; at once they rushed
Together, as two eagles on one prey
Come rushing down together from the clouds,
One from the east, one from the west; their shields
Dashed with a clang together, and a din   475
Rose, such as that the sinewy woodcutters
Make often in the forest's heart at morn,
Of hewing axes, crashing trees, — such blows
Rustum and Sohrab on each other hailed.
And you would say that sun and stars took part   480
In that unnatural conflict: for a cloud
Grew suddenly in heaven, and darked the sun
Over the fighters' heads; and a wind rose
Under their feet, and moaning swept the plain,
And in a sandy whirlwind wrapped the pair.   485

In gloom they twain were wrapped, and they alone;
For both the on-looking hosts on either hand
Stood in broad daylight, and the sky was pure,
And the sun sparkled on the Oxus stream.
But in the gloom they fought, with bloodshot eyes   490
And laboring breath.   First Rustum struck the shield
Which Sohrab held stiff out; the steel-spiked spear
Rent the tough plates, but failed to reach the skin,
And Rustum plucked it back with angry groan.
Then Sohrab with his sword smote Rustum's helm,   495
Nor clove its steel quite through; but all the crest
He shore away, and that proud horse-hair plume,
Never till now defiled, sank to the dust;
And Rustum bowed his head.   But then the gloom
Grew blacker, thunder rumbled in the air   500
And lightenings rent the cloud; and Ruksh the horse,
Who stood at hand, uttered a dreadful cry:
No horse's cry was that, most like the roar
Of some pained desert-lion, who all day
Has trailed the hunter's javelin in his side,   505
And comes at night to die upon the sand;
The two hosts heard that cry, and quaked for fear,
And Oxus curdled as it crossed his stream.
But Sohrab heard, and quailed not, but rushed on,
And struck again; and again Rustum bowed   510
His head; but this time all the blade, like glass,
Sprang in a thousand shivers on the helm,
And in the hand the hilt remained alone.
Then Rustum raised his head; his dreadful eyes
Glared, and he shook on high his menacing spear,   515
And shouted, *Rustum !* Sohrab heard that shout,
And shrank amazed : back he recoiled one step,
And scanned with blinking eyes the advancing form;

And then he stood bewildered, and he dropped
His covering shield, and the spear pierced his side.   520
He reeled, and staggering back sank to the ground.
And then the gloom dispersed, and the wind fell,
And the bright sun broke forth, and melted all
The cloud; and the two armies saw the pair, —
Saw Rustum standing safe upon his feet,   525
And Sohrab wounded on the bloody sand.

Then, with a bitter smile, Rustum began, —
"Sohrab, thou thoughtest in thy mind to kill
A Persian lord this day, and strip his corpse,
And bear thy trophies to Afrasiab's tent;   530
Or else that the great Rustum would come down
Himself to fight, and that thy wiles would move
His heart to take a gift, and let thee go.
And then that all the Tartar host would praise
Thy courage or thy craft, and spread thy fame,   535
To glad thy father in his weak old age.
Fool, thou art slain, and by an unknown man!
Dearer to the red jackals shalt thou be
Than to thy friends, and to thy father old."

And, with a fearless mien, Sohrab replied, —   540
"Unknown thou art, yet thy fierce vaunt is vain.
Thou dost not slay me, proud and boastful man!
No! Rustum slays me, and this filial heart.
For, were I matched with ten such men as thee,
And I were that which till to-day I was,   545
They should be lying here, I standing there.
But that belovèd name unnerved my arm, —
That name, and something, I confess, in thee,
Which troubles all my heart, and made my shield
Fall; and thy spear transfixed an unarmed foe.   550
And now thou boastest and insult'st my fate.

But hear thou this, fierce man, tremble to hear :
The mighty Rustum shall avenge my death !
My father, whom I seek through all the world,
He shall avenge my death, and punish thee !"   555
    As when some hunter in the spring hath found
A breeding eagle sitting on her nest,
Upon the craggy isle of a hill-lake,
And pierced her with an arrow as she rose,
And followed her to find her where she fell   560
Far off ; anon her mate comes winging back
From hunting, and a great way off descries
His huddling young left sole ; at that, he checks
His pinion, and with short uneasy sweeps
Circles above his eyry, with loud screams   565
Chiding his mate back to her nest ; but she
Lies dying, with the arrow in her side,
In some far stony gorge out of his ken,
A heap of fluttering feathers, — never more
Shall the lake glass her, flying over it ;   570
Never the black and dripping precipices
Echo her stormy scream as she sails by, —
As that poor bird flies home, nor knows his loss,
So Rustum knew not his own loss, but stood
Over his dying son, and knew him not.   575
    And with a cold, incredulous voice, he said, —
" What prate is this of fathers and revenge ?
The mighty Rustum never had a son."
    And, with a failing voice, Sohrab replied, —
" Ah, yes, he had ! and that lost son am I.   580
Surely the news will one day reach his ear, —
Reach Rustum, where he sits, and tarries long,
Somewhere, I know not where, but far from here ;
And pierce him like a stab, and make him leap

To arms, and cry for vengeance upon thee. 585
Fierce man, bethink thee, for an only son!
What will that grief, what will that vengeance, be?
Oh, could I live till I that grief had seen!
Yet him I pity not so much, but her,
My mother, who in Ader-baijan dwells 590
With that old king, her father, who grows gray
With age, and rules over the valiant Koords.
Her most I pity, who no more will see
Sohrab returning from the Tartar camp,
With spoils and honor, when the war is done. 595
But a dark rumor will be bruited up,
From tribe to tribe, until it reach her ear;
And then will that defenceless woman learn
That Sohrab will rejoice her sight no more.
But that in battle with a nameless foe, 600
By the far-distant Oxus, he is slain."

  He spoke; and as he ceased he wept aloud,
Thinking of her he left, and his own death.
He spoke; but Rustum listened, plunged in thought.
Nor did he yet believe it was his son 605
Who spoke, although he called back names he knew;
For he had had sure tidings that the babe
Which was in Ader-baijan born to him
Had been a puny girl, no boy at all —
So that sad mother sent him word, for fear 610
Rustum should seek the boy, to train in arms.
And so he deemed that either Sohrab took,
By a false boast, the style of Rustum's son;
Or that men gave it him, to swell his fame.
So deemed he: yet he listened, plunged in thought; 615
And his soul set to grief, as the vast tide
Of the bright rocking ocean sets to shore

At the full moon; tears gathered in his eyes;
For he remembered his own early youth,
And all its bounding rapture; as at dawn,   620
The shepherd from his mountain-lodge descries
A far, bright city, smitten by the sun,
Through many rolling clouds, — so Rustum saw
His youth; saw Sohrab's mother in her bloom;
And that old king, her father, who loved well   625
His wandering guest, and gave him his fair child
With joy; and all the pleasant life they led,
They three, in that long-distant summer-time, —
The castle, and the dewy woods, and hunt
And hound, and morn on those delightful hills   630
In Ader-baijan.   And he saw that youth,
Of age and looks to be his own dear son,
Piteous and lovely, lying on the sand;
Like some rich hyacinth which by the scythe
Of an unskilful gardener has been cut,   635
Mowing the garden grass-plots near its bed,
And lies, a fragrant tower of purple bloom,
On the mown, dying grass, — so Sohrab lay,
Lovely in death, upon the common sand.
And Rustum gazed on him with grief, and said, -   640
   "O Sohrab, thou indeed art such a son
Whom Rustum, wert thou his, might well have loved!
Yet here thou errest, Sohrab, or else men
Have told thee false: thou art not Rustum's son.
For Rustum had no son: one child he had, —   645
But one, — a girl; who with her mother now
Plies some light female task, nor dreams of us, —
Of us she dreams not, nor of wounds, nor war."
   But Sohrab answered him in wrath; for now
The anguish of the deep-fixed spear grew fierce,   650

And he desired to draw forth the steel,
And let the blood flow free, and so to die.
But first he would convince his stubborn foe ;
And, rising sternly on one arm, he said, —
"Man, who art thou who dost deny my words ?   655
Truth sits upon the lips of dying men ;
And falsehood, while I lived, was far from mine.
I tell thee, pricked upon this arm I bear
That seal which Rustum to my mother gave,
That she might prick it on the babe she bore."   660
     He spoke ; and all the blood left Rustum's cheeks,
And his knees tottered, and he smote his hand
Against his breast, his heavy mailèd hand,
That the hard iron corslet clanked aloud ;
And to his heart he pressed the other hand,   665
And in a hollow voice he spake, and said, —
     "Sohrab, that were a proof which could not lie !
If thou show .this, then art thou Rustum's son."
     Then, with weak hasty fingers, Sohrab loosed
His belt, and near the shoulder bared his arm,   670
And showed a sign in faint vermilion points
Pricked ; as a cunning workman, in Pekin,
Pricks with vermilion some clear porcelain vase,
An emperor's gift, — at early morn he paints,
And all day long, and, when night comes, the lamp   675
Lights up his studious forehead and thin hands, —
So delicately pricked the sign appeared
On Sohrab's arm, the sign of Rustum's seal.
It was that griffin which of old reared Zal,
Rustum's great father, whom they left to die,   680
A helpless babe, among the mountain rocks ;
Him that kind creature found, and reared, and loved :
Then Rustum took it for his glorious sign.

And Sohrab bared that image on his arm,
And himself scanned it long with mournful eyes,   685
And then he touched it with his hand, and said, —
  "How say'st thou?   Is that sign the proper sign
Of Rustum's son, or of some other man's?"
  He spoke; but Rustum gazed, and gazed, and stood
Speechless; and then he uttered one sharp cry, —   690
O boy — thy father! and his voice choked there.
And a dark cloud passed before his eyes,
And his head swam, and he sank down to earth.
But Sohrab crawled to where he lay, and cast
His arms about his neck, and kissed his lips,   695
And with fond faltering fingers stroked his cheeks,
Trying to call him back to life; and life
Came back to Rustum, and he oped his eyes,
And they stood wide with horror; and he seized
In both his hands the dust which lay around,   700
And threw it on his head, and smirched his hair, —
His hair, and face, and beard, and glittering arms;
And strong convulsive groanings shook his breast,
And his sobs choked him; and he clutched his sword,
To draw it, and forever let life out.   705
But Sohrab saw his thought, and held his hands,
And with a soothing voice he spake, and said, —
  "Father, forbear! for I but meet to-day
The doom which at my birth was written down
In Heaven, and thou art Heaven's unconscious hand.   710
Surely my heart cried out that it was thou,
When first I saw thee; and thy heart spoke too,
I know it!   But fate trod those promptings down
Under its iron heel; fate, fate engaged
The strife, and hurled me on my father's spear.   715
But let us speak no more of this.   I find

Fat.

My father, let me feel that I have found!
Come, sit beside me on this sand, and take
My head betwixt thy hands, and kiss my cheeks,
And wash them with thy tears, and say, *My son!*   720
Quick, quick! for numbered are my sands of life,
And swift; for like the lightning to this field
I came, and like the wind I go away, —
Sudden, and swift, and like a passing wind;
But it was writ in Heaven that this should be."   725
    So said he; and his voice released the heart
Of Rustum, and his tears broke forth; he cast
His arms round his son's neck, and wept aloud,
And kissed him.   And awe fell on both the hosts,
When they saw Rustum's grief; and Ruksh, the horse,   730
With his head bowing to the ground, and mane
Sweeping the dust, came near, and in mute woe
First to the one, then to the other, moved
His head, as if inquiring what their grief
Might mean; and from his dark, compassionate eyes,   735
The big warm tears rolled down, and caked the sand.
But Rustum chid him with stern voice, and said, —
    "Ruksh, now thou grievest; but, O Ruksh, thy feet
Should then have rotted on their nimble joints,
When first they bore thy master to this field!"   740
    But Sohrab looked upon the horse, and said, —
"Is this, then, Ruksh?   How often, in past days,
My mother told me of thee, thou brave steed,
My terrible father's terrible horse! and said,
That I should one day find thy lord and thee.   745
Come, let me lay my hand upon thy mane!
O Ruksh, thou art more fortunate than I!
For thou hast gone where I shall never go,
And snuffed the breezes of my father's home.

And thou has trod the sands of Seistan,   750
And seen the River of Helmund, and the Lake
Of Zirrah; and the agèd Zal himself
Has often stroked thy neck, and given thee food,
Corn in a golden platter, soaked with wine,
And said, *O Ruksh ! bear Rustum well !*   But I   755
Have never known my grandsire's furrowed face,
Nor seen his lofty house in Seistan,
Nor slaked my thirst at the clear Helmund stream,
But lodged among my father's foes, and seen
Afrasiab's cities only, Samarcand,   760
Bokhara, and lone Khiva in the waste,
And the black Toorkmun tents ; and only drunk
The desert rivers, Moorghab and Tejend,
Kohik, and where the Kalmuks feed their sheep,
The northern Sir ; and this great Oxus stream,   765
The yellow Oxus, by whose brink I die."
     Then, with a heavy groan, Rustum bewailed, —
" Oh that its waves were flowing over me !
Oh that I saw its grains of yellow silt
Roll tumbling in the current o'er my head ! "   770
     But, with a grave mild voice, Sohrab replied, —
" Desire not that, my father ! thou must live.
For some are born to do great deeds, and live
As some are born to be obscured, and die.
Do thou the deeds I die too young to do,   775
And reap a second glory in thine age ;
Thou art my father, and thy gain is mine.
But come !   thou seest this great host of men
Which follow me ; I pray thee, slay not these !
Let me entreat for them : what have they done ?   780
They followed me, my hope, my fame, my star.
Let them all cross the Oxus back in peace.

"Heap a stately mound above my bones,
And plant a far-seen pillar over all."

TOMB OF TAMERLANE, SAMARCAND.

But me thou must bear hence, not send with them
But carry me with thee to Seistan,
And place me on a bed, and mourn for me, —   785
Thou, and the snow-haired Zal, and all thy friends.
And thou must lay me in that lovely earth,
And heap a stately mound above my bones,
And plant a far-seen pillar over all;
That so the passing horseman on the waste   790
May see my tomb a great way off, and cry, —
Sohrab, the mighty Rustum's son, lies there,
Whom his great father did in ignorance kill!
And I be not forgotten in my grave."

  And with a mournful voice, Rustum replied, —   795
" Fear not! as thou hast said, Sohrab my son,
So shall it be: for I will burn my tents,
And quit the host, and bear thee hence with me,
And carry thee away to Seistan,
And place thee on a bed, and mourn for thee,   800
With the snow-headed Zal, and all my friends.
And I will lay thee in that lovely earth,
And heap a stately mound above thy bones,
And plant a far-seen pillar over all,
And men shall not forget thee in thy grave.   805
And I will spare thy host; yea, let them go!
Let them all cross the Oxus back in peace!
What should I do with slaying any more?
For would that all whom I have ever slain
Might be once more alive, — my bitterest foes,   810
And they who were called champions in their time,
And through whose death I won that fame I have, —
And I were nothing but a common man,
A poor, mean soldier, and without renown,
So thou mightest live too, my son, my son!   815

Or rather would that I, even I myself,
Might now be lying on this bloody sand,
Near death, and by an ignorant stroke of thine,
Not thou of mine! and I might die, not thou;
And I, not thou, be borne to Seistan;   820
And Zal might weep above my grave, not thine;
And say, *O son, I weep thee not too sore,*
For willingly, I know, thou met'st thine end!
But now in blood and battles was my youth,
And full of blood and battles is my age,   825
And I shall never end this life of blood."

    Then, at the point of death, Sohrab replied,—
" A life of blood indeed, thou dreadful man!
But thou shalt yet have peace: only not now,
Not yet! but thou shalt have it on that day,   830
When thou shalt sail in a high-masted ship,
Thou and the other peers of Kai Khosroo,
Returning home over the salt blue sea,
From laying thy dear master in his grave."

    And Rustum gazed in Sohrab's face, and said,—   835
" Soon be that day, my son, and deep that sea!
Till then, if fate so wills, let me endure."

    He spoke; and Sohrab smiled on him, and took
The spear, and drew it from his side, and eased
His wound's imperious anguish; but the blood   840
Came welling from the open gash, and life
Flowed with the stream; all down his cold white side
The crimson torrent ran, dim now and soiled,
Like the soiled tissue of white violets
Left, freshly gathered, on their native bank,   845
By children whom their nurses call with haste
Indoors from the sun's eye; his head drooped low,
His limbs grew slack; motionless, white, he lay,—

While, with eyes closed; only when heavy gasps,
Deep heavy gasps quivering through all his frame, 850
Convulsed him back to life, he opened them,
And fixed them feebly on his father's face;
Till now all strength was ebbed, and from his limbs
Unwillingly the spirit fled away,
Regretting the warm mansion which it left, 855
And youth, and bloom, and this delightful world.

So, on the bloody sand, Sohrab lay dead;
And the great Rustum drew his horseman's cloak
Down o'er his face, and sate by his dead son.
As those black granite pillars, once high-reared 860
By Jemshid in Persepolis, to bear
His house, now 'mid their broken flights of steps
Lie prone, enormous, down the mountain side,—
So in the sand lay Rustum by his son.

And night came down over the solemn waste, 865
And the two gazing hosts, and that sole pair,
And darkened all; and a cold fog, with night,
Crept from the Oxus. Soon a hum arose,
As of a great assembly loosed, and fires
Began to twinkle through the fog; for now 870
Both armies moved to camp, and took their meal;
The Persians took it on the open sands
Southward, the Tartars by the river-marge;
And Rustum and his son were left alone.

But the majestic river floated on, 875
Out of the mist and hum of that low land,
Into the frosty starlight, and there moved,
Rejoicing, through the hushed Chorasmian waste,
Under the solitary moon; he flowed
Right for the Polar star, past Orgunjè, 880
Brimming, and bright, and large; then sands begin

To hem his watery march, and dam his streams,
And split his currents ; that for many a league
The shorn and parcelled Oxus strains along
Through beds of sand and matted rushy isles, —   885
Oxus, forgetting the bright speed he had
In his high mountain cradle in Pamere,
A foiled circuitous wanderer, — till at last
The longed-for dash of waves is heard, and wide
His luminous home of waters opens, bright   890
And tranquil, from whose floor the new-bathed stars
Emerge, and shine upon the Aral Sea.

ALFRED, LORD TENNYSON

ENOCH ARDEN.

Three children of three houses.

ENOCH ARDEN.

Long lines of cliff breaking have left a chasm;
And in the chasm are foam and yellow sands;
Beyond, red roofs about a narrow wharf
In cluster; then a moulder'd church; and higher
A long street climbs to one tall-tower'd mill;   5
And high in heaven behind it a gray down
With Danish barrows; and a hazelwood,
By autumn nutters haunted, flourishes
Green in a cuplike hollow of the down.

Here on this beach a hundred years ago,   10
Three children of three houses, Annie Lee,
The prettiest little damsel in the port,
And Philip Ray the miller's only son,
And Enoch Arden, a rough sailor's lad
Made orphan by a winter shipwreck, play'd   15
Among the waste and lumber of the shore,
Hard coils of cordage, swarthy fishing-nets,
Anchors of rusty fluke, and boats updrawn;
And built their castles of dissolving sand
To watch them overflow'd, or following up   20
And flying the white breaker, daily left
The little footprint daily wash'd away.

A narrow cave ran in beneath the cliff :
In this the children play'd at keeping house.
Enoch was the host one day, Philip the next,   25
While Annie still was mistress ; but at times
Enoch would hold possession for a week :
" This is my house and this is my little wife."
" Mine too " said Philip " turn and turn about : "
When, if they quarrell'd, Enoch stronger-made   30
Was master : then would Philip, his blue eyes
All flooded with the helpless wrath of tears,
Shriek out " I hate you, Enoch," and at this
The little wife would weep for company,
And pray them not to quarrel for her sake,   35
And say she would be little wife to both.

But when the dawn of rosy childhood past,
And the new warmth of life's ascending sun
Was felt by either, either fixed his heart
On that one girl ; and Enoch spoke his love,   40
But Philip loved in silence ; and the girl
Seem'd kinder unto Philip than to him ;
But she loved Enoch ; tho' she knew it not,
And would if ask'd deny it.   Enoch set
A purpose evermore before his eyes,   45
To hoard all savings to the uttermost,
To purchase his own boat, and make a home
For Annie : and so prosper'd that at last
A luckier or a bolder fisherman,
A carefuller in peril, did not breathe   50
For leagues along that breaker-beaten coast
Than Enoch.   Likewise had he served a year
On board a merchantman, and made himself
Full sailor ; and he thrice had pluck'd a life

From the dread sweep of the down-streaming seas: 55
And all men look'd upon him favorably :
And ere he touch'd his one-and-twentieth May,
He purchased his own boat, and made a home
For Annie, neat and nestlike, halfway up
The narrow street that clamber'd toward the mill. 60

Then, on a golden autumn eventide,
The younger people making holiday,
With bag and sack and basket, great and small,
Went nutting to the hazels.   Philip stay'd
(His father lying sick and needing him) 65
An hour behind ; but as he climb'd the hill,
Just where the prone edge of the wood began
To feather toward the hollow, saw the pair,
Enoch and Annie, sitting hand-in-hand,
His large gray eyes and weather-beaten face 70
All-kindled by a still and sacred fire,
That burn'd as on an altar.   Philip look'd,
And in their eyes and faces read his doom ;
Then, as their faces drew together, groan'd,
And slipt aside, and like a wounded life 75
Crept down into the hollows of the wood ;
There, while the rest were loud in merrymaking,
Had his dark hour unseen, and rose and past
Bearing a lifelong hunger in his heart.

   So these were wed, and merrily rang the bells, 80
And merrily ran the years, seven happy years,
Seven happy years of health and competence,
And mutual love and honorable toil ;
With children ; first a daughter.   In him woke,
With his first babe's first cry, the noble wish 85

To save all earnings to the uttermost,
And give his child a better bringing-up
Than his had been, or hers ; a wish renew'd,
When two years after came a boy to be
The rosy idol of her solitudes,   90
While Enoch was abroad on wrathful seas,
Or often journeying landward ; for in truth
Enoch's white horse, and Enoch's ocean-spoil
In ocean-smelling osier, and his face,
Rough-redden'd with a thousand winter gales,   95
Not only to the market-cross were known,
But in the leafy lanes behind the down,
Far as the portal-warding lion-whelp,
And peacock-yewtree of the lonely Hall,
Whose Friday fare was Enoch's ministering.   100

   Then came a change, as all things human change.
Ten miles to northward of the narrow port
Open'd a larger haven : thither used
Enoch at times to go by land or sea ;
And once when there, and clambering on a mast   105
In harbor, by mischance he slipped and fell :
A limb was broken when they lifted him ;
And while he lay recovering there, his wife
Bore him another son, a sickly one :
Another hand crept too across his trade   110
Taking her bread and theirs : and on him fell,
Altho' a grave and staid God-fearing man,
Yet lying thus inactive, doubt and gloom.
He seem'd, as in a nightmare of the night,
To see his children leading evermore   115
Low miserable lives of hand-to-mouth,
And her, he loved, a beggar : then he pray'd

"Save them from this, whatever comes to me."
And while he pray'd, the master of that ship
Enoch had served in, hearing his mischance,   120
Came, for he knew the man and valued him,
Reporting of his vessel China-bound,
And wanting yet a boatswain.   Would he go?
There yet were many weeks before she sail'd,
Sail'd from this port.   Would Enoch have the place?   125
And Enoch all at once assented to it,
Rejoicing at that answer to his prayer.

So now that shadow of mischance appear'd
No graver than as when some little cloud
Cuts off the fiery highway of the sun,   130
And isles a light in the offing: yet the wife —
When he was gone — the children — what to do?
Then Enoch lay long-pondering on his plans;
To sell the boat — and yet he loved her well —
How many a rough sea had he weather'd in her!   135
He knew her, as a horseman knows his horse —
And yet to sell her — then with what she brought
Buy goods and stores — set Annie forth in trade
With all that seamen needed or their wives —
So might she keep the house while he was gone.   140
Should he not trade himself out yonder? go
This voyage more than once? yea twice or thrice
As oft as needed — last, returning rich,
Become the master of a larger craft,
With fuller profits lead an easier life,   145
Have all his pretty young ones educated,
And pass his days in peace among his own.

Thus Enoch in his heart determined all :
Then moving homeward came on Annie pale,

Nursing the sickly babe, her latest-born.   150
Forward she started with a happy cry,
And laid the feeble infant in his arms ;
Whom Enoch took, and handled all his limbs,
Appraised his weight and fondled fatherlike,
But had no heart to break his purposes   155
To Annie, till the morrow, when he spoke.

Then first since Enoch's golden ring had girt
Her finger, Annie fought against his will :
Yet not with brawling opposition she,
But manifold entreaties, many a tear,   160
Many a sad kiss by day by night renew'd
(Sure that all evil would come out of it)
Besought him, supplicating, if he cared
For her or his dear children, not to go.
He not for his own self caring but her,   165
Her and her children, let her plead in vain ;
So grieving held his will, and bore it thro'.

For Enoch parted with his old sea-friend,
Bought Annie goods and stores, and set his hand
To fit their little streetward sitting-room   170
With shelf and corner for the goods and stores.
So all day long till Enoch's last at home,
Shaking their pretty cabin, hammer and axe,
Auger and saw, while Annie seem'd to hear
Her own death-scaffold raising, shrill'd and rang,   175
Till this was ended, and his careful hand, —
The space was narrow, — having order'd all
Almost as neat and close as Nature packs
Her blossom or her seedling, paused ; and he,
Who needs would work for Annie to the last,   180
Ascending tired, heavily slept till morn.

Besought him, supplicating, if he cared
For her or his dear children, not to go.

And Enoch faced this morning of farewell
Brightly and boldly.   All his Annie's fears,
Save, as his Annie's, were a laughter to him.
Yet Enoch as a brave God-fearing man   185
Bow'd himself down, and in that mystery
Where God-in-man is one with man-in-God,
Pray'd for a blessing on his wife and babes
Whatever came to him : and then he said
" Annie, this voyage by the grace of God   190
Will bring fair weather yet to all of us.
Keep a clean hearth and a clear fire for me,
For I'll be back, my girl, before you know it."
Then lightly rocking baby's cradle "and he,
This pretty, puny, weakly little one, —   195
Nay — for I love him all the better for it —
God bless him, he shall sit upon my knees
And I will tell him tales of foreign parts,
And make him merry, when I come home again.
Come, Annie, come, cheer up before I go."   200

Him running on thus hopefully she heard,
And almost hoped herself ; but when he turn'd
The current of his talk to graver things
In sailor fashion roughly sermonizing
On providence and trust in Heaven, she heard,   205
Heard and not heard him ; as the village girl,
Who sets her pitcher underneath the spring,
Musing on him that used to fill it for her,
Hears and not hears, and lets it overflow.

At length she spoke " O Enoch, you are wise.   210
And yet for all your wisdom well know I
That I shall look upon your face no more."

" Well then," said Enoch " I shall look on yours.
Annie, the ship I sail in passes here
(He named the day) ; get you a seaman's glass,   215
Spy out my face, and laugh at all your fears."

But when the last of those last moments came,
" Annie, my girl, cheer up, be comforted,
Look to the babes, and till I come again
Keep everything shipshape, for I must go.   220
And fear no more for me ; or if you fear
Cast all your cares on God ; that anchor holds.
Is He not yonder in those uttermost
Parts of the morning ? if I flee to these
Can I go from Him ? and the sea is His,   225
The sea is His : He made it."

                                 Enoch rose,
Cast his strong arms about his drooping wife,
And kiss'd his wonder-stricken little ones ;
But for the third, the sickly one, who slept
After a night of feverous wakefulness,   230
When Annie would have raised him Enoch said
" Wake him not ; let him sleep ; how should the child
Remember this ? " and kissed him in his cot.
But Annie from her baby's forehead clipt
A tiny curl, and gave it : this he kept   235
Thro' all his future ; but now hastily caught
His bundle, waved his hand, and went his way.

She, when the day that Enoch mention'd, came,
Borrow'd a glass, but all in vain : perhaps
She could not fix the glass to suit her eye ;   240
Perhaps her eye was dim, hand tremulous ;

She saw him not : and while he stood on deck
Waving, the moment and the vessel past.

  Ev'n to the last dip of the vanishing sail
She watch'd it and departed weeping for him ;   245
Then, tho' she mourn'd his absence as his grave,
Set her sad will no less to chime with his,
But throve not in her trade, not being bred
To barter, nor compensating the want
By shrewdness, neither capable of lies,   250
Nor asking overmuch and taking less,
And still foreboding " what would Enoch say ? "
For more than once, in days of difficulty
And pressure, had she sold her wares for less
Than what she gave in buying what she sold :   255
She fail'd and sadden'd knowing it ; and thus,
Expectant of that news which never came,
Gain'd for her own a scanty sustenance,
And lived a life of silent melancholy.

  Now the third child was sickly-born and grew   260
Yet sicklier, tho' the mother cared for it
With all a mother's care : nevertheless,
Whether her business often call'd her from it,
Or thro' the want of what it needed most,
Or means to pay the voice who best could tell   265
What most it needed — howso'e'er it was,
After a lingering, — ere she was aware, —
Like the caged bird escaping suddenly,
The little innocent soul flitted away.

  In that same week when Annie buried it,   270
Philip's true heart, which hunger'd for her peace

(Since Enoch left he had not look'd upon her),
Smote him, as having kept aloof so long.
"Surely," said Philip, "I may see her now,
May be some little comfort;" therefore went,   275
Past thro' the solitary room in front,
Paused for a moment at an inner door,
Then struck it thrice, and, no one opening,
Enter'd; but Annie, seated with her grief,
Fresh from the burial of her little òne,   280
Cared not to look on any human face,
But turn'd her own toward the wall and wept.
Then Philip standing up said falteringly
"Annie, I came to ask a favor of you."

He spoke; the passion in her moan'd reply   285
"Favor from one so sad and so forlorn
As I am!" half abash'd him; yet unask'd,
His bashfulness and tenderness at war,
He set himself beside her, saying to her:

"I came to speak to you of what he wish'd,   290
Enoch, your husband: I have ever said
You chose the best among us — a strong man:
For where he fixt his heart he set his hand
To do the thing he will'd, and bore it thro'.
And wherefore did he go this weary way,   295
And leave you lonely? not to see the world —
For pleasure? — nay, but for the wherewithal
To give his babes a better bringing-up
Than his had been, or yours: that was his wish.
And if he come again, vext will he be   300
To find the precious morning hours were lost.
And it would vex him even in his grave,

If he could know his babes were running wild
Like colts about the waste.   So, Annie, now —
Have we not known each other all our lives ?   305
I do beseech you by the love you bear
Him and his children not to say me nay —
For, if you will, when Enoch comes again
Why then he shall repay me — if you will,
Annie — for I am rich and well-to-do.   310
Now let me put the boy and girl to school :
This is the favor that I came to ask."

   Then Annie with her brows against the wall
Answer'd " I cannot look you in the face ;
I seem so foolish and so broken down.   315
When you came in, my sorrow broke me down ;
And now I think your kindness breaks me down ;
But Enoch lives ; that is borne in on me :
He will repay you : money can be repaid ;
Not kindness such as yours."

                              And Philip ask'd   320
" Then you will let me, Annie ? "

                              There she turn'd,
She rose, and fixt her swimming eyes upon him,
And dwelt a moment on his kindly face,
Then calling down a blessing on his head
Caught at his hand, and rung it passionately,   325
And past into the little garth beyond
So lifted up in spirit he moved away.

   Then Philip put the boy and girl to school,
And bought them needful books, and every way,

Like one who does his duty by his own,   330
Made himself theirs ; and tho' for Annie's sake,
Fearing the lazy gossip of the port,
He oft denied his heart his dearest wish,
And seldom crost her threshold, yet he sent
Gifts by the children, garden-herbs and fruit,   335
The late and early roses from his wall,
Or conies from the down, and now and then,
With some pretext of fineness in the meal
To save offence of charitable, flour
From his tall mill that whistled on the waste.   340

But Philip did not fathom Annie's mind :
Scarce could the woman when he came upon her,
Out of full heart and boundless gratitude
Light on a broken word to thank him with.
But Philip was her children's all-in-all ;   345
From distant corners of the street they ran
To greet his hearty welcome heartily ;
Lords of his house and of his mill were they ;
Worried his passive ear with petty wrongs
Or pleasures, hung upon him, play'd with him   350
And call'd him Father Philip.   Philip gain'd
As Enoch lost ; for Enoch seem'd to them
Uncertain as a vision or a dream,
Faint as a figure seen in early dawn
Down at the far end of an avenue,   355
Going we know not where : and so ten years,
Since Enoch left his hearth and native land,
Fled forward, and no news of Enoch came.

It chanced one evening Annie's children long'd
To go with others nutting to the wood,   360

And Annie would go with them; then they begg'd
For Father Philip (as they call'd him) too:
Him, like the working bee in blossom-dust,
Blanch'd with his mill, they found; and saying to him
"Come with us Father Philip" he denied; 365
But when the children pluck'd at him to go,
He laugh'd, and yielded readily to their wish,
For was not Annie with them? and they went.

But after scaling half the weary down,
Just where the prone edge of the wood began 370
To feather toward the hollow, all her force
Fail'd her; and sighing, "Let me rest," she said:
So Philip rested with her well-content;
While all the younger ones with jubilant cries
Broke from their elders, and tumultuously 375
Down thro' the whitening hazels made a plunge
To the bottom, and dispersed, and bent or broke
The lithe reluctant boughs to tear away
Their tawny clusters, crying to each other
And calling, here and there, about the wood. 380

But Philip sitting at her side forgot
Her presence, and remember'd one dark hour
Here in this wood, when like a wounded life
He crept into the shadow: at last he said,
Lifting his honest forehead, "Listen, Annie, 385
How merry they are down yonder in the wood.
Tired, Annie?" for she did not speak a word.
"Tired?" but her face had fall'n upon her hands;
At which, as with a kind of anger in him,
"The ship was lost," he said, "the ship was lost! 390
No more of that! why should you kill yourself

And make them orphans quite ? "   And Annie said
" I thought not of it : but — I know not why —
Their voices make me feel so solitary."

   Then Philip coming somewhat closer spoke.   395
" Annie, there is a thing upon my mind,
And it has been upon my mind so long,
That tho' I know not when it first came there,
I know that it will out at last.   O Annie,
It is beyond all hope, against all chance,   400
That he who left you ten long years ago
Should still be living ; well then — let me speak :
I grieve to see you poor and wanting help :
I cannot help you as I wish to do
Unless — they say that women are so quick —   405
Perhaps you know what I would have you know —
I wish you for my wife.   I fain would prove
A father to your children : I do think
They love me as a father : I am sure
That I love them as if they were mine own ;   410
And I believe, if you were fast my wife,
That after all these sad uncertain years,
We might be still as happy as God grants
To any of his creatures.   Think upon it :
For I am well-to-do — no kin, no care,   415
No burthen, save my care for you and yours :
And we have known each other all our lives,
And I have loved you longer than you know."

   Then answer'd Annie ; tenderly she spoke :
" You have been as God's good angel in our house.   420
God bless you for it, God reward you for it,
Philip, with something happier than myself.

"I am content," he answer'd, "to be loved
A little after Enoch."

Can one love twice? can you be ever loved
As Enoch was? what is it that you ask?"
"I am content," he answer'd, "to be loved   425
A little after Enoch."   "O," she cried,
Scared as it were, "dear Philip, wait a while:
If Enoch comes — but Enoch will not come —
Yet wait a year, a year is not so long:
Surely I shall be wiser in a year: 430
O wait a little!"   Philip sadly said
"Annie, as I have waited all my life
I well may wait a little."   "Nay," she cried,
"I am bound: you have my promise — in a year:
Will you not bide your year as I bide mine?"   435
And Philip answer'd "I will bide my year."

  Here both were mute, till Philip glancing up
Beheld the dead flame of the fallen day
Pass from the Danish barrow overhead;
Then fearing night and chill for Annie, rose   440
And sent his voice beneath him thro' the wood.
Up came the children laden with their spoil;
Then all descended to the port, and there
At Annie's door he paused and gave his hand,
Saying gently "Annie, when I spoke to you,   445
That was your hour of weakness.   I was wrong,
I am always bound to you, but you are free."
Then Annie weeping answer'd "I am bound."

  She spoke; and in one moment as it were,
While yet she went about her household ways,   450
Ev'n as she dwelt upon his latest words,
That he had loved her longer than she knew,
That autumn into autumn flash'd again.

And there he stood once more before her face,
Claiming her promise. "Is it a year?" she ask'd. **455**
"Yes, if the nuts," he said, "be ripe again:
Come out and see." But she — she put him off —
So much to look to — such a change — a month —
Give her a month — she knew that she was bound —
A month — no more. Then Philip with his eyes **460**
Full of that lifelong hunger, and his voice
Shaking a little like a drunkard's hand,
"Take your own time, Annie, take your own time."
And Annie could have wept for pity of him:
And yet she held him on delayingly **465**
With many a scarce-believable excuse,
Trying his truth and his long-sufferance,
Till half-another year had slipt away.

By this the lazy gossips of the port,
Abhorrent of a calculation crost, **470**
Began to chafe as at a personal wrong.
Some thought that Philip did but trifle with her;
Some that she but held off to draw him on;
And others laugh'd at her and Philip too,
As simple folk that knew not their own minds, **475**
And one, in whom all evil fancies clung
Like serpent eggs together, laughingly
Would hint at worse in either. Her own son
Was silent, tho' he often look'd his wish;
But evermore the daughter prest upon her **480**
To wed the man so dear to all of them
And lift the household out of poverty;
And Philip's rosy face contracting grew
Careworn and wan; and all these things fell on her
Sharp as reproach.

At last one night it chanced 485
That Annie could not sleep, but earnestly
Pray'd for a sign "my Enoch, is he gone?"
Then compass'd round by the blind wall of night
Brook'd not the expectant terror of her heart,
Started from bed, and struck herself a light, 490
Then desperately seized the holy Book,
Suddenly set it wide to find a sign,
Suddenly put her finger on the text,
" Under the palm-tree." That was nothing to her :
No meaning there : she closed the Book and slept : 495
When lo ! her Enoch sitting on a height,
Under a palm-tree, over him the Sun :
" He is gone," she thought, " he is happy, he is singing
Hosanna in the highest : yonder shines
The Sun of Righteousness, and these be palms 500
Whereof the happy people strowing cried
' Hosanna in the highest !' " Here she woke,
Resolved, sent for him and said wildly to him
" There is no reason why we should not wed."
" Then for God's sake," he answered, " both our sakes, 505
So you will wed me, let it be at once."

So these were wed and merrily rang the bells,
Merrily rang the bells and they were wed.
But never merrily beat Annie's heart.
A footstep seem'd to fall beside her path, 510
She knew not whence ; a whisper on her ear,
She knew not what ; nor loved she to be left
Alone at home, nor ventured out alone.
What ail'd her then, that ere she enter'd, often
Her hand dwelt lingeringly on the latch, 515
Fearing to enter : Philip thought he knew :

Such doubts and fears were common to her state,
Being with child : but when her child was born,
Then her new child was as herself renew'd,
Then the new mother came about her heart,   520
Then her good Philip was her all-in-all,
And that mysterious instinct wholly died.

    And where was Enoch ? prosperously sail'd
The ship " Good Fortune," tho' at setting forth
The Biscay, roughly riding eastward, shook   525
And almost overwhelm'd her, yet unvext
She slipped across the summer of the world,
Then after a long tumble about the Cape,
And frequent interchange of foul and fair,
She passing thro' the summer world again,   530
The breath of heaven came continually
And sent her sweetly by the golden isles,
Till silent in her oriental haven.

    There Enoch traded for himself, and bought
Quaint monsters for the market of those times,   535
A gilded dragon, also, for the babes.

    Less lucky her home-voyage : at first indeed
Thro' many a fair sea-circle, day by day,
Scarce-rocking, her full-busted figure-head
Stared o'er the ripple feathering from her bows :   540
Then follow'd calms, and then winds variable,
Then baffling, a long course of them ; and last
Storm, such as drove her under moonless heavens
Till hard upon the cry of " breakers " came
The crash of ruin, and the loss of all   545
But Enoch and two others.   Half the night,

Buoy'd upon floating tackle and broken spars,
These drifted, stranding on an isle at morn
Rich, but the loneliest in a lonely sea.

No want was there of human sustenance,   550
Soft fruitage, mighty nuts, and nourishing roots;
Nor save for pity was it hard to take
The helpless life so wild that it was tame.
There in a seaward-gazing mountain-gorge
They built, and thatch'd with leaves of palm, a hut,   555
Half hut, half native cavern.   So the three,
Set in this Eden of all plenteousness,
Dwelt with eternal summer, ill-content.

For one, the youngest, hardly more than boy,
Hurt in that night of sudden ruin and wreck,   560
Lay lingering out a five-years' death-in-life.
They could not leave him.   After he was gone,
The two remaining found a fallen stem ;
And Enoch's comrade, careless of himself,
Fire-hollowing this in Indian fashion, fell   565
Sun-stricken, and that other lived alone.
In those two deaths he read God's warning " wait."

The mountain wooded to the peak, the lawns
And winding glades high up like ways to Heaven,
The slender coco's drooping crown of plumes,   570
The lightning flash of insect and of bird,
The luster of the long convolvuluses
That coil'd around the stately stems, and ran
Ev'n to the limit of the land, the glows
And glories of the broad belt of the world,   575
All these he saw; but what he fain had seen

He could not see, the kindly human face,
Nor ever hear a kindly voice, but heard
The myriad shriek of wheeling ocean-fowl,
The league-long roller thundering on the reef,   580
The moving whisper of huge trees that branch'd
And blossom'd in the zenith, or the sweep
Of some precipitous rivulet to the wave,
As down the shore he ranged, or all day long
Sat often in the seaward-gazing gorge,   585
A shipwreck'd sailor, waiting for a sail:
No sail from day to day, but every day
The sunrise broken into scarlet shafts
Among the palms and ferns and precipices ;
The blaze upon the waters to the east ;   590
The blaze upon his island overhead ;
The blaze upon the waters to the west ;
Then the great stars that globed themselves in Heaven,
The hollower-bellowing ocean, and again
The scarlet shafts of sunrise — but no sail.   595

There often as he watch'd or seem'd to watch,
So still, the golden lizard on him paused,
A phantom made of many phantoms moved
Before him haunting him, or he himself
Moved haunting people, things and places, known   600
Far in a darker isle beyond the line ;
The babes, their babble, Annie, the small house,
The climbing street, the mill, the leafy lanes,
The peacock-yewtree and the lonely Hall,
The horse he drove, the boat he sold, the chill   605
November dawns and dewy-glooming downs,
The gentle shower, the smell of dying leaves,
And the low moan of leaden-color'd seas.

There often as he watch'd or seem'd to watch,
So still, the golden lizard on him paused.

She wanted water.

Once likewise, in the ringing of his ears,
Tho' faintly, merrily — far and far away —   610
He heard the pealing of his parish bells;
Then, tho' he knew not wherefore, started up
Shuddering, and when the beauteous hateful isle
Return'd upon him, had not his poor heart
Spoken with That, which being everywhere   615
Lets none, who speaks with Him, seem all alone,
Surely the man had died of solitude.

Thus over Enoch's early-silvering head
The sunny and rainy seasons came and went
Year after year.   His hopes to see his own,   620
And pace the sacred old familiar fields,
Not yet had perish'd, when his lonely doom
Came suddenly to an end.   Another ship
(She wanted water) blown by baffling winds,
Like the Good Fortune, from her destined course,   625
Stay'd by this isle, not knowing where she lay:
For since the mate had seen at early dawn
Across a break on the mist-wreathen isle
The silent water slipping from the hills,
They sent a crew that landing burst away   630
In search of stream or fount, and fill'd the shores
With clamor.   Downward from his mountain-gorge
Stept the long-hair'd, long-bearded solitary,
Brown, looking hardly human, strangely clad,
Muttering and mumbling, idiotlike it seem'd   635
With inarticulate rage, and making signs
They knew not what: and yet he led the way
To where the rivulets of sweet water ran;
And ever as he mingled with the crew,
And heard them talking, his long-bounden tongue   640

Was loosen'd, till he made them understand;
Whom, when their casks were fill'd, they took aboard.
And there the tale he utter'd brokenly,
Scarce-credited at first but more and more,
Amazed and melted all who listen'd to it ·   645
And clothes they gave him and free passage home;
But oft he work'd among the rest and shook
His isolation from him.   None of these
Came from his country, or could answer him,
If question'd, aught of what he cared to know.   650
And dull the voyage was with long delays,
The vessel scarce sea-worthy; but evermore
His fancy fled before the lazy wind
Returning, till beneath a clouded moon
He like a lover down thro' all his blood   655
Drew in the dewy meadowy morning-breath
Of England, blown across her ghostly wall;
And that same morning officers and men
Levied a kindly tax upon themselves,
Pitying the lonely man, and gave him it: 660
Then moving up the coast they landed him,
Ev'n in that harbor whence he sail'd before.

    There Enoch spoke no word to any one,
But homeward — home — what home? had he a home?
His home, he walk'd.   Bright was that afternoon,   665
Sunny but chill; till drawn thro' either chasm,
Where either haven open'd on the deeps,
Roll'd a sea-haze and whelm'd the world in gray;
Cut off the length of highway on before,
And left but narrow breadth to left and right   670
Of wither'd holt or tilth or pasturage.
On the nigh-naked tree the robin piped

Disconsolate, and thro' the dripping haze
The dead weight of the dead leaf bore it down.
Thicker the drizzle grew, deeper the gloom;   675
Last, as it seem'd, a great mist-blotted light
Flared on him, and he came upon the place.

Then down the long street having slowly stolen,
His heart foreshadowing all calamity,
His eyes upon the stones, he reach'd the home   680
Where Annie lived and loved him, and his babes
In those far-off seven happy years were born;
But finding neither light nor murmur there
(A bill of sale gleam'd thro' the drizzle) crept
Still downward thinking "dead or dead to me!"   685

Down to the pool and narrow wharf he went,
Seeking a tavern which of old he knew,
A front of timber-crost antiquity,
So propt, worm eaten, ruinously old,
He thought it must have gone; but he was gone   690
Who kept it; and his widow Miriam Lane,
With daily-dwindling profits held the house;
A haunt of brawling seamen once, but now
Stiller, with yet a bed for wandering men.
There Enoch rested silent many days.   695

But Miriam Lane was good and garrulous,
Nor let him be, but often breaking in,
Told him, with other annals of the port,
Not knowing — Enoch was so brown, so bow'd,
So broken — all the story of his house.   700
His baby's death, her growing poverty,
How Philip put her little ones to school.

And kept them in it, his long wooing her,
Her slow consent, and marriage, and the birth
Of Philip's child : and o'er his countenance   705
No shadow past, nor motion : any one,
Regarding, well had deem'd he felt the tale
Less than the teller : only when she closed
" Enoch, poor man, was cast away and lost "
He, shaking his gray head pathetically,   710
Repeated muttering " cast away and lost ; "
Again in deeper inward whispers " lost ! "

    But Enoch yearn'd to see her face again ;
" If I might look on her sweet face again
And know that she is happy."   So the thought   715
Haunted and harass'd him, and drove him forth,
At evening when the dull November day
Was growing duller twilight, to the hill.
There he sat down gazing on all below ;
There did a thousand memories roll upon him,   720
Unspeakable for sadness.   By and by
The ruddy square of comfortable light,
Far-blazing from the rear of Philip's house,
Allured him, as the beacon-blaze allures
The bird of passage, till he madly strikes   725
Against it, and beats out his weary life.

    For Philip's dwelling fronted on the street,
The latest house to landward ; but behind,
With one small gate that open'd on the waste,
Flourish'd a little garden square and wall'd :   730
And in it throve an ancient evergreen,
A yewtree, and all round it ran a walk
Of shingle, and a walk divided it :

But Enoch yearn'd to see her face again.

But Enoch shunn'd the middle walk and stole
Up by the wall, behind the yew; and thence   735
That which he better might have shunn'd, if griefs
Like his have worse or better, Enoch saw.

For cups and silver on the burnish'd board
Sparkled and shone; so genial was the hearth:
And on the right hand of the hearth he saw   740
Philip, the slighted suitor of old times,
Stout, rosy, with his babe across his knees;
And o'er her second father stoopt a girl,
A later but a loftier Annie Lee,
Fair-hair'd and tall, and from her lifted hand   745
Dangled a length of ribbon and a ring
To tempt the babe, who rear'd his creasy arms,
Caught at and ever miss'd it, and they laugh'd;
And on the left hand of the hearth he saw
The mother glancing often toward her babe,   750
But turning now and then to speak with him,
Her son, who stood beside her tall and strong,
And saying that which pleased him, for he smiled.

Now when the dead man come to life beheld
His wife his wife no more, and saw the babe   755
Hers, yet not his, upon the father's knee,
And all the warmth, the peace, the happiness,
And his own children tall and beautiful,
And him, that other, reigning in his place,
Lord of his rights and of his children's love, —   760
Then he, tho' Miriam Lane had told him all,
Because things seen are mightier than things heard,
Stagger'd and shook, holding the branch, and fear'd
To send abroad a shrill and terrible cry,

Which in one moment, like the blast of doom,   765
Would shatter all the happiness of the hearth.

  He therefore turning softly like a thief,
Lest the harsh shingle should grate underfoot,
And feeling all along the garden-wall,
Lest he should swoon and tumble and be found,   770
Crept to the gate, and open'd it, and closed,
As lightly as a sick man's chamber-door,
Behind him, and came out upon the waste.

  And there he would have knelt, but that his knees
Were feeble, so that falling prone he dug   775
His fingers into the wet earth and pray'd.

  " Too hard to bear ! why did they take me thence ?
O God Almighty, blessed Savior, Thou
That didst uphold me on my lonely isle,
Uphold me, Father, in my loneliness   780
A little longer ! aid me, give me strength
Not to tell her, never to let her know.
Help me not to break in upon her peace.
My children too ! must I not speak to these ?
They know me not.   I should betray myself.   785
Never : No father's kiss for me — the girl
So like her mother, and the boy, my son."

  There speech and thought and nature fail'd a little,
And he lay tranced ; but when he rose and paced
Back toward his solitary home again,   790
All down the long and narrow street he went
Beating it in upon his weary brain,

As tho' it were the burthen of a song,
" Not to tell her, never to let her know."

He was not all unhappy.   His resolve   795
Upbore him, and firm faith, and evermore
Prayer from a living source within the will,
And beating up thro' all the bitter world,
Like fountains of sweet water in the sea,
Kept him a living soul.   " This miller's wife,"   800
He said to Miriam, " that you spoke about,
Has she no fears that her first husband lives ? "
" Ay, ay, poor soul," said Miriam, " fear enow !
If you could tell her you had seen him dead,
Why, that would be her comfort ; " and he thought   · 805
" After the Lord has call'd me she shall know,
I wait his time," and Enoch set himself,
Scorning an alms, to work whereby to live.
Almost to all things could he turn his hand.
Cooper he was and carpenter, and wrought   810
To make the boatmen fishing-nets, or help'd
At lading and unlading the tall barks,
That brought the stinted commerce of those days ;
Thus earn'd a scanty living for himself ;
Yet since he did but labor for himself,   815
Work without hope, there was not life in it
Whereby the man could live ; and as the year
Roll'd itself round again to meet the day
When Enoch had return'd, a languor came
Upon him, gentle sickness, gradually   820
Weakening the man, till he could do no more,
But kept the house, his chair, and last his bed.
And Enoch bore his weakness cheerfully.
For sure no gladlier does the stranded wreck

See thro' the gray skirts of a lifting squall   825
The boat that bears the hope of life approach
To save the life despair'd of, than he saw
Death dawning on him, and the close of all.

    For thro' that dawning gleam'd a kindlier hope
On Enoch thinking "after I am gone,   830
Then may she learn I lov'd her to the last,"
He call'd aloud for Miriam Lane and said
" Woman, I have a secret — only swear,
Before I tell you — swear upon the book
Not to reveal it, till you see me dead."   835
" Dead," clamor'd the good woman, " hear him talk !
I warrant, man, that we shall bring you round."
" Swear," added Enoch sternly, " on the book."
And on the book, half-frighted, Miriam swore.
Then Enoch rolling his gray eyes upon her,   840
" Did you know Enoch Arden of this town ? "
" Know him ? " she said, " I knew him far away.
Ay, ay, I mind him coming down the street ;
Held his head high, and cared for no man, he."
Slowly and sadly Enoch answer'd her ;   845
"His head is low, and no man cares for him.
I think I have not three days more to live ;
I am the man."   At which the woman gave
A half-incredulous, half-hysterical cry.
" You Arden, you ! nay, — sure he was a foot   850
Higher than you be."   Enoch said again
" My God has bow'd me down to what I am ;
My grief and solitude have broken me ;
Nevertheless, know you that I am he
Who married — but that name has twice been changed —
I married her who married Philip Ray.   856

Sit, listen." Then he told her of his voyage,
His wreck, his lonely life, his coming back,
His gazing in on Annie, his resolve,
And how he kept it. As the woman heard, 860
Fast flow'd the current of her easy tears,
While in her heart she yearn'd incessantly
To rush abroad all round the little haven,
Proclaiming Enoch Arden and his woes ;
But awed and promise-bounden she forbore, 865
Saying only, " See your bairns before you go !
Eh, let me fetch 'em, Arden," and arose
Eager to bring them down, for Enoch hung
A moment on her words, but then replied :

" Woman, disturb me not now at the last, 870
But let me hold my purpose till I die.
Sit down again ; mark me and understand,
While I have power to speak. I charge you now,
When you shall see her, tell her that I died
Blessing her, praying for her, loving her ; 875
Save for the bar between us, loving her
As when she laid her head beside my own.
And tell my daughter Annie, whom I saw
So like her mother, that my latest breath
Was spent in blessing her and praying for her. 880
And tell my son that I died blessing him.
And say to Philip that I blest him too ;
He never meant us anything but good.
But if my children care to see me dead,
Who hardly knew me living, let them come, 885
I am their father ; but she must not come,
For my dead face would vex her after-life.
And now there is but one of all my blood

Who will embrace me in the world-to-be :
This hair is his : she cut it off and gave it,   890
And I have borne it with me all these years,
And thought to bear it with me to my grave ;
But now my mind is changed, for I shall see him,
My babe in bliss : wherefore when I am gone,
Take, give her this, for it may comfort her :   895
It will moreover be a token to her,
That I am he."

        He ceased ; and Miriam Lane
Made such a voluble answer promising all,
That once again he roll'd his eyes upon her
Repeating all he wish'd, and once again   900
She promised.

        Then the third night after this,
While Enoch slumber'd motionless and pale,
And Miriam watch'd and dozed at intervals,
There came so loud a calling of the sea,
That all the houses in the haven rang.   905
He woke, he rose, he spread his arms abroad
Crying with a loud voice "A sail ! a sail !
I am saved" ; and so fell back and spoke no more.

So passed the strong heroic soul away.
And when they buried him the little port   910
Had seldom seen a costlier funeral.

NOTES.

(Numbers refer to lines.)

THE RIME OF THE ANCIENT MARINER.

The Ancient Mariner was published in *Lyrical Ballads* in 1798. Its title was *The Rime of the Ancyent Marinere in Seven Parts*. In the second edition of *Lyrical Ballads* (1800) this was changed to *The Ancient Mariner, a Poet's Reverie*. The text was much altered from the original, and the extremely archaic spelling was modernized. The texts of 1802 and 1805 were essentially the same as that of 1800. In 1817 the ballad was reprinted in *Sybylline Leaves*, with a Latin motto and some textual changes. In this edition the marginal gloss was added and the grotesquely horrible element was made less prominent. An argument, or introduction, prefixed to the edition of 1798, was omitted in the succeeding editions until that of 1817, when it was restored.

The occasion of *Lyrical Ballads* has been related by both Coleridge and Wordsworth, each giving some details omitted by the other. Wordsworth tells us that the book grew out of a plan intended to furnish them with money for defraying the expenses of a walking tour among the Quantock Hills. The sum needed was £5, but the work soon more than sufficed to raise that amount. The slender anonymous volume did more than any other book to restore the romantic element to English verse.

In *Biographia Literaria* Coleridge has recorded the poetic principles on which *Lyrical Ballads* is based. In conversation with Wordsworth they frequently discussed "the two cardinal points of poetry, the power of exciting the sympathy of the reader by a faithful adherence to the truth of nature, and the power of giving the interest of novelty by the modifying colors of the imagination." It was decided to compose a series of poems of two sorts. "In one the incidents and agents were to be, in part at least, supernatural; and the excellence aimed at was to consist in the interesting of the affections by the dramatic truth of such emotions as would naturally accompany such situations, supposing them real. For the second class, subjects were to be chosen from ordinary life; the characters and incidents were to be such as will be found in every village and its vicinity where there is a meditative and feeling mind to seek after them or to notice them when they present themselves."

Thus originated the plan of *Lyrical Ballads*. Coleridge undertook the supernatural and romantic parts, while Wordsworth contributed the incidents from common life. *The Ancient Mariner* was the only poem that Coleridge furnished, though he began *Christabel* and *The Dark Ladie*, "in which," he says, "I should have more nearly realized my ideal than I had done in my first attempt."

The source of the plot has been the subject of numerous conjectures. According to Coleridge, the story was founded on the dream of a friend. This dream, however, was merely the germ of the idea; the working of the poet's imagination, the influence of his wide and varied reading, gradually molded the poem into something altogether his own. In Shevlock's *Voyages* occurs a passage describing the albatrosses observed as the ship was doubling Cape Horn. Wordsworth suggested that the "old navigator" be represented as having killed one of the birds, and that the tutelary spirit of that region seek vengeance upon him for the crime. Another book which may have had some influence is Captain Thomas James's *Strange and Dangerous Voyage*, published in London in 1633. Still another theory is that the poet gained his idea from a letter of the fourth century recounting the "astounding wonders concerning the shipwreck of an old man." He is described as the sole survivor from the crews of a numerous fleet, a "crew of Angels" navigated his ship, and the "Pilot of the World" steered the vessel to the Lucanian Shore." Investigation of this nature, however, is perhaps more curious than useful; we may enjoy the wonderful imaginative beauty of the poem without knowledge of its origins.

Whatever the occasion or source of the ballad may have been, the fact remains that *The Ancient Mariner* is one of the most remarkable creations in all literature. The general attitude of criticism is well shown by a few lines from James Russell Lowell:

"It is enough for us here that he (Coleridge) has written some of the most poetical poetry in the language, and one poem, *The Ancient Mariner*, not only unparalleled, but unapproached in its kind, and that kind of the rarest. . . . Coleridge has taken the old ballad measure and given to it, by an indefinable charm wholly his own, all the sweetness, all the melody and compass, of a symphony. And how picturesque it is in the proper sense of the word. I know nothing like it. There is not a description in it. It is all picture. Descriptive poets generally confuse us with multiplicity of detail; we cannot see their forest for trees; but Coleridge never errs in this way. With instinctive tact he touches the right chord of association, and is satisfied as we also are. I should find it hard to explain the singular charm of his diction, there is so much nicety of art and purpose in it, whether for music or for meaning. . . . The words seem common words enough, but in the order of them, in the choice, variety, and position of the vowel sounds, they become magical. The most decrepit vocable in the language throws away its crutches to dance and sing at his piping. . . . More bits of Coleridge have imbedded themselves in my memory than of any other poet who delighted my youth, unless I should except the sonnets of Shakespeare. This argues perfectness of expression."

The total impression of the poem has been summarized thus:

"*The Ancient Mariner* is the baseless fabric of a vision. We are put under a spell, like the wedding guest, and carried off to the isolation and remoteness of mid-ocean. Through the chinks of the narrative the wedding music sounds unreal and far off. What may not happen to a man alone on a wide, wide sea? The line between earthly and unearthly vanishes. Did the mariner really see the spectral bark and hear spirits talking, or was it all but the phantasmagoria of the calenture, the fever that attacks the sailor on the tropic main, so that he seems to see green meadows and water brooks on the level brine? No one can tell; for he is himself the only witness, and the ship is sunk at the harbor mouth. One conjectures that no wreckers or divers will ever bring it to the top again. Nay, was not the mariner, too, a specter? Now he is gone, and what was all this that he told me, thinks the wedding guest, as he rises on the morrow morn. Or did he tell me, or did I only dream it? A light shadow cast by some invisible thing swiftly traverses the sunny face of nature and is gone. Did we see it, or imagine it? Even so elusive, so uncertain, so shadowy and phantom-like is the spiriting of this wonderful poem."

Speaking of the technique of the poem, Wordsworth said : "The versification is harmonious and exquisitely varied, exhibiting the utmost powers of the ballad meter and every variety of which it is capable." The well-known "ballad stanza" adopted by Coleridge consists of four lines, alternately three and four feet, and rhymed in the second and fourth lines. But the freedom with which this old measure is handled constitutes much of the peculiar charm of *The Ancient Mariner.*

Thus, the poet does not confine himself to four lines; we find six- and eight-line stanzas, and a few even of nine lines, where the thought gains both in beauty and effectiveness from being treated at greater length. To understand the point, read lines 45–50, the whole stanza formed by lines 203–11, or the exquisite simile contained in the stanza beginning with line 367. A study of the metrical forms will reveal the extraordinary skill displayed by Coleridge. Every device known to the ballad type is used in the poem. Two other points may be mentioned. The first is "internal rhyme," which appears frequently, and of which a fine example is the passage beginning "The fair breeze blew, the white foam flew" (line 103). The second point is the use of alliteration, to illustrate which we may cite the lines,

> "Alone, alone, all, all alone,
>   Alone on a wide, wide sea."

The diction is entirely in keeping with the spirit of the old ballad literature. Archaic words are employed, such as "eftsoon," "clift," "swound," "uprist," to produce the right ballad effect. In the first edition of *The Ancient Mariner* this archaic usage was much more freely employed, but the later issues tended to suggest and not directly to imitate the ancient methods. Extreme simplicity of phrase is also characteristic of the diction —

> "The sun came up upon the left,
>   Out of the sea came he."

> "The silly buckets on the deck,
>   That had so long remained,
> I dreamt that they were filled with dew,
>   And when I awoke, it rained."

But whether the diction be archaic or artless, it suits itself marvelously to the atmosphere of old times in which the scene of the action is laid.

2. **one of three**: Throughout the poem the prevailing numbers are three, five, seven, and nine. The odd numbers have always been regarded as fitting to the supernatural — the nine muses, the three fates, etc. There are three Witches in *Macbeth*, and one of them sings,

> "Thrice to mine and thrice to thine,
> And thrice again to make up nine.
> Peace, the charm's wound up."

8. **the feast is set**: Can you see why a wedding is chosen to form the natural background of the poem? Walter Pater says (*Appreciations*, p. 101) that the unity of this poem is secured in part by the skill with which the incidents of the wedding feast are made to break in dreamily from time to time upon the main story.

11. **loon**: Cf. *Macbeth*, V. 3. 1–2.

12. **Eftsoons**: immediately, at once. An obsolete word, introduced to give an archaic flavor to the poem.

15–16. These lines were furnished by Wordsworth.

23. **kirk**: church. Note how the shore-line gradually disappears as the ship sails farther from land. " As the ship leaves the harbor, the dropping from sight first of the kirk, then of the hill, finally of the lighthouse top, gives a condensed picture of a North Devonshire harbor town, with its church and cluster of houses nestled in a cleft of the steep hills that overhang the sea."

25. **upon the left**, because the ship was heading south. Coleridge is careful to indicate the position of the ship from time to time. Due south she sails into the South Polar seas, where we are to suppose she is saved from the ice by the Albatross. Then she steers north before the south wind, until she is becalmed in the tropics, and is met by the specter ship. The Mariner's vessel is then "moved onward from beneath" by the Polar Spirit. They reach the equator,

> "The Sun, right up above the mast,
> Had fixed her to the ocean."

The struggle between the Polar Spirit seeking vengeance for the death of the albatross, and the Guardian Saint is shown by the " short, uneasy motion " of the ship. Finally the Polar Spirit is satisfied by the promise that the Mariner " penance more must do," and the ship sails on.

29. **Higher and higher,** etc. : because the ship is sailing south into the tropics.

32. **bassoon** : a deep-toned wind instrument. The merriment of the wedding is contrasted with the grim tale of the Ancient Mariner.

36. **minstrelsy** : band of musicians, leading the wedding party to the banquet.

45–50. One of the fine similes for which the poem is famous.

53. **ice, mast-high,** etc. : Captain James, *North-West Passage :* " All this day we did beat and were beaten fearfully amongst the ice, it blowing a very storm.   In the evening were inclosed amongst great pieces, as high as our poop ; and some of the sharp blue corners of them did reach quite under us.   We had ice not far off about us, and some pieces as high as our topmast head."

51–62.   Travelers in the Polar regions have commented upon the accuracy of this description. Fog and snow, followed by ice, are familiar features of those sections.

55. **clifts** : old form of " cliffs." It survives in our modern " cleft."

62. **swound** : swoon, dream.

63. **Albatross** : a sea-bird of great strength and beauty, native to the Antarctic Ocean. Shevlock, in his *Voyages*, speaks thus : " These were accompanied by albatrosses, the largest sort of sea fowls, some of them extending their wings 12 or 13 feet." The incident of the Albatross was suggested by Wordsworth. Of his part in the poem he said : " Much the greatest part of the story was Mr. Coleridge's invention ; but certain parts I suggested. . . . As we endeavored to proceed conjointly . . . our respective manners proved so widely different that it would have been quite presumptuous in me to do anything but separate from an undertaking upon which I could only have been a clog."

76. **vespers nine** : that is, for nine days. " Vespers " was the evening service repeated in churches.

79–82. The bond of fellowship between man and animal is broken ; moreover, the Albatross had saved the ship. The crime, involving cruelty and ingratitude, is committed and punishment must follow. Wanton cruelty is a sin that calls for vengeance. We must be careful, however, not to insist too closely upon the "moral" of the poem. It is to be read for its imaginative beauty and its metrical charm — in a word, as poetry.

83. **upon the right**: the ship is now heading north.

91–102. The uncertainty of the sailors is typical of the ignorant, who are influenced in their opinions by mere external circumstances.

98. **uprist**: obsolete form for "uprose."

104. In *Sybylline Leaves* (1817) this line reads:

"The furrow streamed off free."

The following note was added by Coleridge: " I had not long been on board a ship before I perceived that this was the image as seen from the shore, or from another vessel. From the ship itself the wake appears like a brook flowing off from the stern." The earlier reading reappeared in subsequent editions. It is certainly more euphonious, and Coleridge was evidently willing to allow the unimportant inaccuracy in order to gain a greater beauty of expression.

106. Although Coleridge's marginal gloss here mentions the Pacific, it would seem that the poet had in mind the Sargasso Sea. If this be so, the general description which follows is more true and the further movement of the voyage to his own country becomes more appropriate.

125–6. The testimony of a sailor bears witness to the truth of Coleridge's imaginative picture: " Next day, and for a whole week after, we had a stark calm — such a calm as one realizes who reads sympathetically that magical piece of work, the ' Ancient Mariner.' What an amazing instance of the triumph of the human imagination ! For Coleridge certainly never witnessed such a scene as he there describes with an accuracy of detail that is astounding. Very few sailors have noticed the sickening condition of the ocean when the life-giving breeze totally fails for any length of time, or, if they have, they have said but little about it. Of course, some parts of the sea show the evil effects of stagnation much sooner than others; but, generally speaking, want of wind at sea, if long continued, produces a condition of things dangerous to the health of any land nearby." F. T. Bullen, in *The Cruise of the Cachelot.*

141–2. This is what we call " poetic justice," *i.e.*, the punishment is fitted to the crime. Note that the " cross " is the sign of deliverance from sin, whereas the Albatross is the sign of the sin itself. Note, too, that each part of the poem, except the last, closes with some reference to the Albatross, or the penance, or the sin.

143. Instances of ships being becalmed for days and even weeks at a time were, of course, common in Coleridge's day. The era of steam had not yet arrived.

152. **I wist**: old form for " I know." A corruption of the Anglo-Saxon adverb *gewiss*, certainly.

155. **sprite**: spirit.

164. The word **grin** is here used with peculiar suggestiveness. The face is distorted, the muscles drawn with the agony of thirst. In *Table Talk* (May 31, 1830), Coleridge writes : " I took the thought of *grinning for joy* from my companion's remark to me when we had climbed to the top of Plimlimmon, and were fairly dead with thirst. We could not speak from constriction till we found a little puddle under a stone. He said to me, ' You grinned like an idiot ! ' He had done the same."

168. **work us weal**: do us good, help us. The word " weal " is obsolete, surviving only in " weal-th," and the proverbial " in weal or woe."

178. **Heaven's Mother** : Mary, Queen of Heaven — *Regina Coeli.*

184. **gossameres** : cobwebs, poetic form of " gossamer." Note the exact observation in " restless gossameres."

185. At this point Coleridge deliberately adds such details as will make the picture more ghastly. In the first edition (*Lyrical Ballads*) the following stanza is found :

> "*His* bones were black with many a crack,
>   All black and bare, I ween ;
> Jet-black and bare, save where with rust
> Of mouldy damps and charnel crust
> They're patch'd with purple and green."

The last two lines of the next stanza read, —

> " And she is far liker Death than he ;
>   Her flesh makes the still air cold."

Can you give any reason for the change? Coleridge, commenting on Milton's description of Death (*Paradise Lost*, Book II, lines 666 ff.), remarks : " The grandest efforts of poetry are when the imagination is called forth to produce, not a distinct form, but a strong working of the mind, still offering what is still repelled, and again creating what is again rejected ; the result being what the poet wishes to impress, viz., the substitution of a sublime feeling of the unimaginable for mere images."

192. **white as leprosy** : See II Kings, V. 27.

193. The Nightmare Life-in-Death diced with Death for the soul of the Ancient Mariner. The former won, and the fate of the wanderer was to live under the doom of telling his tale " at an uncertain hour."

199–200. The rapid coming of darkness is characteristic of the Tropics.

203–5. A wonderful suggestion of extreme fear. **sideways**, as of one expecting a blow without any idea where it is to come from.

209. **clomb** : archaic form of " climbed." **the eastern bar** : the horizon.

226–7. These lines are Wordsworth's.

232–62. These stanzas express what Coleridge called " the sublime feeling of the unimaginable," to show the horror undergone by the Ancient Mariner in punishment for his crime.

263. From here to the end of the section, the feeling gradually changes from horror to the sensations of beauty and peace. At last the Ancient Mariner is moved to a spirit of love for the " happy living things," and his curse passes from him. Read the beautiful marginal gloss on lines 257–71.

292–6. An excellent example of " onomatopœia." Coleridge expresses the comfort and refreshment of sleep by the sound of the words as well as by their meaning.

297. **silly** : empty, useless.

302. **dank** : sodden, drenched.

310. **anear** : poetic form of " near."

312. **sere** : worn with age. The word is now spelt *sear*. The literal meaning is dry, or withered, as in Shakespeare's

> " my way of life
> Is fallen into the sear, the yellow leaf."

There seems to be always the connotation of old age. It is an interesting question whether in Coleridge's usage there is not a suggestion of a long space of time having elapsed during the voyage, so that the sailor who started out a young man has at the end become the " ancient mariner " with his long gray beard and skinny hand. The ship, too, grows old and worn, so that the Hermit notices her " warped planks " and the weather-beaten sails hanging like " brown skeletons of leaves " (lines 530, 533). The conception of a long passage of time imposed by supernatural means occurs in several mediæval legends, and has been preserved to our own day in the familiar tale of Rip Van Winkle.

314. **sheen:** brilliant, shining. In line 56 the word is used as a noun.

317. **wan:** pale, because dimmed by the " fire-flags."

319. **sedge:** water-weeds on a river-bank.

338. **wont:** accustomed.

358-72. These stanzas are some of the most melodious in all poetry. For pure beauty of sound and loveliness of suggestion it is difficult to find anything more charming than the lines 369-72. Swinburne had in mind such a passage as this when he wrote: "Of Coleridge's best verses I venture to affirm that the world has nothing like them, and can never have."

362. **jargoning:** confused melody.

377. **nine fathom deep:** a " fathom " is six feet; the expression here, however, is used merely to suggest great depth.

379. **the spirit:** see line 132.

382. Note the accent of " also," intentionally reminiscent of the old ballad meter.

383. **The Sun,** etc.: They are now on the equator, and the Polar Spirit has no power north of the line. He attempts to hold the ship, but the kindly Guardian Saint wins her for the homeward voyage.

386-8. The " echo " effect here was afterwards much used by Edgar Allan Poe, a great admirer of Coleridge and temperamentally not unlike him.

394. I cannot say, I do not know.

399. A common form of oath used in the ballads.

404-5. The cruelty and ingratitude of the Ancient Mariner is here indicated.

419. A reference to the movement of the tides, which are caused by the influence of the moon.

435. **charnel-dungeon**: a " charnel-house," in mediæval times, was the place where the dead body was placed before the actual burial.

443. **the ocean green**: that is, the natural, wholesome sea, as contrasted with the terrible region where the ship had been held so long. The Ancient Mariner is returning to the world of reality.

446–51. A fine poetical interpretation of an experience known to most persons. In Lamb's essay *Witches and Other Night Fears* this stanza is quoted, and comment is made upon Coleridge's imaginative power.

464–7. Cf. lines 21–24.

467. A typical ballad line.

472. " How pleasantly, how reassuringly, the whole nightmare story is made to end among the clear, fresh sounds and lights of the bay where it began." The lines from 472 to 480 are filled with a peculiar beauty of calm and moonlight. Note, in particular, the phrases, " clear as glass," " shadow of the Moon," " white with silent light," and the supreme touch

> " The moonlight steeped in silentness
> The steady weathercock."

489. A familiar ballad oath.

490–5. Wordsworth suggested this incident. The good spirits come to help the Ancient Mariner. They signal the land, and the Pilot rows out to take the ship into port.

498–9. The underlying thought has never been so finely expressed.

501. **cheer**: the Pilot hails the ship.

507. **blast**: destroy. Cf. *Hamlet*, I. l. 127:

> " I'll cross it, though it blast me."

512. **shrieve my soul**: absolve me from my sin. " Shrieve " is an obsolete form of " shrive."

517–9. Note the typical ballad line-ending.

517–8. The archaic spelling should be noted.

524. **trow**: vow, declare.

525. **lights**: cf. lines 494–5.

526. **that** is the subject of **made**.

529. **warped**: twisted, bent — here, from age. The ship has been long at sea.

530. **sere**: again the age of the ship is emphasized, as in lines 312 and 529.

535. **ivy-tod**: bush, thick mass of growing foliage.

536. **the wolf below**, etc.: This casual mention of wolves is introduced to suggest the old-time setting of the story.

549. **The ship went down like lead**: The ship has been a stage for the enacting of strange and terrible things; its disappearance frees the Ancient Mariner from the records of his sin. We know now that it was a magic ship, such as can never be seen again, and we turn from the region of mystery to that of human reality.

558–9. A fine poetic suggestion of an echo.

575. Made the sign of the cross, to protect himself from evil.

591. With the close of the wonderful tale, the actual world once more bursts upon us.

595. **vesper-bell**: bell for evening service.

597–600. Cf. lines 232–5.

621. **Turned from the bridegroom's door**: Why?

623. **forlorn**: bereft, deprived.

624. **sadder**: more serious, more thoughtful.

The conclusion of the poem suggests the spirit of universal love. The opinion of Coleridge with regard to this " moral " element may be judged from a remark in his *Table Talk:* " Mrs. Barbauld once told me that she admired *The Ancient Mariner* very much, but that there were two faults in it, — it was improbable and had no moral. As to the probability, I owned that that might admit some question, but as to the want of moral, I told her that in my judgment the poem had too much ; and that the only or chief fault, if I might say so, was the obtrusion of the moral sentiment so openly on the reader, as a principle or cause of action in a work of such pure imagination. It ought to have had no more moral than the Arabian Nights Tales."

A summary of the thought which underlies the poem, in so far as it yields itself to summarizing, will be helpful to the student.

Part I contains a " statement of the problem " — if so unimaginative a phrase can be applied to a highly imaginative piece of writing. The Ancient Mariner has destroyed the harmony between nature and man by killing the albatross. To Coleridge such an act was treason against the laws of life.

Part II shows the companions of the Ancient Mariner involved in his sufferings. They curse him, and as a reminder of his sin hang the dead albatross about his neck.

Part III depicts the Ancient Mariner as the prey of Life-in-Death. He is separated by Death from his companions.

Part IV gives a vivid picture of the agony suffered by the Ancient Mariner, when

> " The sky and the sea, and the sea and the sky
>   Lay like a load on my weary eye
>   And the dead were at my feet.''

All Nature is against him. But at last, unselfishly, he cries out in admiration of the happy living things in the sea —

> " I blessed them unaware.''

Then the curse is loosed ; he is again at one with life.

Part V relates how Nature now works for the release of the Ancient Mariner, but the consequences of his sin are still felt. Even his companions cannot really live.

Part VI. Here we have the return to normal life. Yet the Ancient Mariner " has penance more '' to do.

Part VII. The sin of the Ancient Mariner is forgiven, but not forgotten. He must still work out his fate — for " no man liveth unto himself.'' He is doomed to " pass like night from land to land,'' and tell his tale.

TYPICAL PASSAGES FROM THE ANCIENT MARINER.

> The bride hath paced into the hall,
> Red as a rose is she ;
> Nodding their heads before her, goes
> The merry minstrelsy.

> The ship was cheered, the harbor cleared
> Merrily did we drop
> Below the kirk, below the hill,
> Below the lighthouse top.

As who pursued with yell and blow
Still treads the shadow of his foe,
And forward bends his head.

And now there came both mist and snow,
And it grew wondrous cold,
And ice, mast-high, came floating by,
As green as emerald.

The fair breeze blew, the white foam flew,
The furrow followed free;
We were the first that ever burst
Into that silent sea.

Day after day, day after day,
We stuck, nor breath nor motion;
As idle as a painted ship
Upon a painted ocean.

Water, water, everywhere,
And all the boards did shrink;
Water, water, everywhere,
Nor any drop to drink.

The Nightmare Life-in-Death was she,
Who thicks men's blood with cold.

The Sun's rim dips; the stars rush out:
At one stride comes the dark.

Fear at my heart, as at a cup,
My lifeblood seemed to sip!

Alone, alone, all, all alone,
Alone on a wide, wide sea!

O happy living things! no tongue
Their beauty might declare:
A spirit of love gushed from my heart,
And I blessed them unaware!

O sleep! it is a gentle thing,
Beloved from pole to pole!

Sometimes a dropping from the sky
I heard the skylark sing;
Sometimes all little birds that are,
How they seemed to fill the sea and air
With their sweet jargoning!

An angel's song,
That makes the heavens be mute.

It ceased; yet still the sails made on
A pleasant noise till noon,
A noise like of a hidden brook
In the leafy month of June,
That to the sleeping woods all night
Singeth a quiet tune.

Still as a slave before his lord,
The Ocean hath no blast;
His great bright eye most silently
Up to the Moon is cast.

Like one that on a lonesome road
Doth walk in fear and dread,
And having once turned round walks on,
And turns no more his head,
Because he knows a frightful fiend
Doth close behind him tread.

The moonlight steeped in silentness
The steady weathercock.

The bay was white with silent light.

No voice did they impart, —
No voice; but oh! the silence sank
Like music on my heart.

All was still, save that the hill
Was telling of the sound.

This soul hath been
Alone on a wide, wide sea:
So lonely 'twas, that God himself
Scarce seemed there to be.

He prayeth best who loveth best
All things, both great and small;
For the dear God who loveth us,
He made and loveth all.

QUESTIONS AND TOPICS FOR DISCUSSION BASED ON THE ANCIENT MARINER.

1. Make a list of the archaic words used by Coleridge. Why are such words employed? Discuss their poetic value.
2. The supernatural element in the poem.
3. Trace the dominating motive in each of the seven divisions.
4. Give some instances of the use of metaphor and simile. Is their chief function to develop the thought, or to increase the beauty of the poem?
5. Select, forming your judgment by oral reading, some passages which are marked by charm of melody. Investigate Coleridge's use of " onomatopœia," the poetic device wherein the sound of the words reflects the meaning.
6. In what respects does Coleridge modify the typical ballad form in the course of the poem? If you are familiar with any of the old ballads, indicate the chief points of resemblance and difference. Characteristic ballads are: *Sir Patrick Spens*, *The Hunting of the Cheviot*, or any of the *Robin Hood* cycle.
7. What use is made by Coleridge of natural scenery? Compare his nature-pictures with those of Wordsworth in such poems as *Tintern Abbey*, the *Immortality Ode*, or *The Daffodils*.
8. Can you explain why Wordsworth, as he tells us, withdrew from taking part in the composition of *The Ancient Mariner?* What would have been the result, in your opinion, of a continued association of the two poets in this instance?
9. The " pictures " in the poem. How are they made effective?
10. Why is the " merry din " of the wedding feast suggested at intervals?

11. How does the poet emphasize the ideas of loneliness — of horror — of thirst — of peace after suffering?

12. Cite two or three passages which seem to you characteristic of Coleridge's poetic style. In what do you find their strongest appeal?

13. What did Coleridge mean by saying that, in his opinion, the poem had " too much " moral? Do you agree with this view?

14. Of the close of *The Ancient Mariner* a critic has said: " This unexpected gentle conclusion brings our feet back to the common soil with a bewildered sweetness of relief and soft quiet after the prodigious strain of mental excitement."
Write a careful explanatory comment upon this statement.

15. Explain, or comment upon, the following:
" There was a ship," quoth he. Listens like a three-years' child. A dismal sheen. Noises in a swound. A witch's oils. They for joy did grin. To work us weal. White as leprosy. The star-dogged Moon. The silly buckets. For a charnel dungeon fitter. I viewed the ocean green. The harbor bay was clear as glass. He loves to talk with marineres. The hill was telling of the sound. Of sense forlorn.

SOHRAB AND RUSTUM.

In *Sohrab and Rustum* Arnold has been careful to observe the traditions of Epic poetry. The epic is defined as a long narrative poem, written in stately verse, in which the events are grouped about some great central figure — usually a god or a hero. The plot is simple and the action moves forward by a series of episodes. Epic poems usually have a national significance, or are in some way typical of national life and experience. The great epics are: Greek, Homer's *Iliad* and *Odyssey;* Roman, Vergil's *Æneid;* Italian, Dante's *Divine Comedy;* Anglo-Saxon, *Beowulf;* English, Milton's *Paradise Lost.* Of Arnold's poem a critic has said that it is " the nearest analogue in English to the plainness of thought, plainness of diction, and nobleness of Homer."

Further resemblances may be pointed out, whereby the epic spirit is preserved. There are many fine pictures in the poem —

notably, for example, the opening passage, and lines 334–40. The similes, too, are typical; one would especially instance the noble lines about the eagle (lines 556–75), which constitute one of the most beautiful similes in the English language. Typical, also, is the deliberate description of the single combat — the speeches, and the telling of each blow given. Finally, we should note the " objectivity " of the whole poem — the manner, that is, in which the poet's personality is kept in the background, and the action carried to its conclusion without comment made or moral drawn. All these qualities are Homeric. And the noble descriptive passage at the close serves excellently to leave upon our minds the impression of a classic purity of style.

The poem is based upon a single episode in the *Shah Nameh,* or " Book of Kings," the great Persian epic written by the poet Firdusi in the tenth century. In the main, Arnold has closely followed the original, but in minor details he has adapted the " tale of tears," as the episode is called, to his own needs.

Rustum, son of Zal, is the hero of *Shah Nameh.* During one of his many expeditions he married a beautiful maiden named Tamineh, but was soon called away to a fresh adventure. Sohrab, their son, was born after Rustum left. The mother, fearing that her boy would be taken from her, sent word to Rustum that the child was a girl. As Sohrab grew up he learned that the mighty Rustum was his father and determined to find him began a search through the wide world.

> " I seek one man, one man, and one alone, —
>   Rustum, my father; who I hoped should greet,
>   Should one day greet, upon some well-fought field,
>   His not unworthy, not inglorious, son."

Arnold's poem opens at the time when the Tartars have invaded Persia; among them the bravest champion is Sohrab. To round out and complete the story, Arnold modified it here and there.

1. **And**: This word emphasizes the episodic character of the poem. It is used in the sense of " to continue the narrative."

2. **Oxus**: now called the Amoo Darya. Compare these lines with those which complete the poem, 875 to the end. " The introduction

of the tranquil pictures of the Oxus, both at the beginning and close of the poem, flowing steadily on, unmoved by the tragedy which has been enacted on her shore, forms one of the most artistic features in the setting of the story."   The Oxus rises in the Pamir table-land, in a lake 15,000 feet above sea level, and flows northwest into the Aral Sea. Its length is 1300 miles.

3. **Tartar**: This is the general name for the nomadic tribes that inhabit Central Asia and Southern Russia. The Kalmuck tribe, celebrated by De Quincey in *The Flight of a Tartar Tribe,* is one of them. The Tartars were a fierce and warlike people; hence the expression " he caught a Tartar."

11. **Peran-Wisa** was a Turanian chief and the general of King Afrasiab's forces. Iran, the Persian empire, was separated from Turania by the Oxus.

12. The comparative luxury of the Persians, as compared to the plain living of the hardy Tartars, is suggested in line 192.

13. **bee-hives**: in allusion to the characteristic shape of the Tartar tents.

15. **Pamere**: a table-land 16,000 feet high, north of Afghanistan. The natives call it " the roof of the world."

19. In summer the land was flooded.

23. **felts**: skins specially prepared.

38. **Afrasiab** was king of the Turanians and had many Tartar tribes among his forces (see lines 119–34). In the old legends he was said to be as strong as a lion and his shadow to extend for miles. At the time of the episode described in our poem the great power of Afrasiab was waning. The house of Zal (Rustum's father) had pledged itself to expel the invaders. This promise was fulfilled through the prowess of Rustum, who defeated Afrasiab and compelled his retreat across the Oxus.

40. **Samarcand**: a city in what is now Russian Turkestan. It is to-day a center of Mohammedan culture and learning.

42. **Ader-baijan** (*Azer-biyan*): a province on the northwest frontier of Persia, near Turania.

49. Here is the motive that furnishes the tragic element of the story.

82. **Seistan**: Pronounced in three syllables — Se-is-tan. A Province of Afghanistan, containing a lake of the same name. **Zal,**

Rustum's father, was said to be descended from Benjamin, son of David. When he was born his hair was snow-white, and Saum, his father, left him to die in the mountains. He was found and cared for, however, by a "griffin," a creature half lion and half eagle, which carried him away to its nest. Here he was safely kept until his father repented and took him home again.

85. Cf. lines 226–7.

86–91. Peran-Wisa's solicitude for Sohrab is an invention of Arnold's. Why is it introduced?

92. **ravening**: searching for prey.

94–104. This passage is conceived in the true epic manner. The attention to detail — the interest of the poet in a vivid picture — is characteristic of all great epic poems. For another example, see lines 265–70.

99. **ruler's staff**: emblem of leadership used on a peaceful mission. See II Kings IV. 29.

101. **Kara-Kul** was about 30 miles southwest of Bokhara, and was noted for the fine quality of its fleeces.

107. **Haman**: second-in-command, after Peran-Wisa.

110–40. This "geographical" passage is typical of the epic style. Such name-lists appear in the *Iliad* and the *Æneid*, and may readily be found in Milton's *Paradise Lost* — see Book I, lines 376–521, Book XI, lines 385–411. Arnold is careful to select in this passage names which not only possess historical significance, but which also in themselves have musical sound. Most of the places mentioned may be found on maps of Afghanistan, Turkestan, or Persia.

113. **Casbin**: a fortified city on the old caravan route from Persia to Europe.

114. **Elburz**: a mountain north of Casbin, forming the "divide" between the Persian plateau and the Caspian Sea.

Aralian estuaries: river-mouths along the Aral Sea.

115. **frore**: frozen. Cf. Milton, *Paradise Lost*, Book II, lines 594–5:

> ". . . the parched air
> Burns frore, and cold performs the effect of fire."

119. **Bokhara**: a region of Central Asia.

120. **Khiva**: a province in the valley of the lower Oxus, southeast of Bokhara.

ferment the milk of mares : " An intoxicating drink, *koumiss* made of camel's or mare's milk, is in wide use among the steppe tribes."

121. **Toorkmuns :** our modern " Turcomans," a branch of the Turkish race found chiefly in northern Persia and Afghanistan.

122. **Tukas :** soldiers from the provinces of Ader-baijan.

123. **Attruck :** a river running west in Khorassan and emptying into the Caspian Sea.

128. **Ferghana :** a province of Turkestan.

129. **Jaxartes :** the old name of the Sir Daria river, which flows north from the Pamir into the Aral Sea.

131. **Kipchack :** a province south of Khiva, on the Oxus river.

132. **Kalmucks :** a nomadic tribe of the Mongolian race, living in western Siberia.

Kuzzaks : the " Cossacks " of the Russian steppes, a warlike people of uncertain origin.

133. **Kirghizzes :** a wild tribe related both to the Mongols and Tartars, and dwelling in northern Turkestan.

138. **Khorassan :** " The land of the sun " — a desert province of northeastern Persia.

Ilyats : irregular soldiers, or " levies."

147. **fixed :** halted, drew up.

154–6. One of the numerous fine similes which add so greatly to the beauty and significance of the poem. See, for other examples, lines 302–8, 556–75. Such similes are typical of the epic style. Compare the famous lines in *Paradise Lost,* Book I, lines 589–600 :

" He above the rest
Stood like a tower ; his form had not yet lost
All her original brightness, nor appeared
Less than archangel ruined, and the excess
Of glory obscured : as when the sun new ris'n
Looks through the horizontal misty air
Shorn of his beams, or from behind the moon
In dim eclipse disastrous twilight sheds
On half the nations, and with fear of change
Perplexes monarchs. Dark'n'd so, yet shone
Above them all the Archangel."

The two similes of lines 154–69 serve to indicate in a very vivid way the effect of the challenge upon the two armies.

156. corn: here used in the English sense of "grain." In America the word has come to mean Indian corn, or "maize."

160. Cabool: The capital of Afghanistan; an important mercantile center.

161. Indian Caucasus: The "Hindoo Koosh" mountains, a lofty range north of Cabool, forming the boundary between Turkestan and Afghanistan.

173. The King: Kai Khosroo — see lines 223–4.

178–9. The picture of Rustum sullenly abiding in his tent brings to mind the similar attitude of Achilles in the *Iliad*, Book I.

200. falcon: a species of hawk, carefully trained for catching game birds.

217. Iran's chiefs: Persian chiefs. The Persians called their country Iran. Tradition says that the Persians and the Turks were descended from two brothers, Iran and Turan.

221. Go to! An expletive, common in Elizabethan English, equivalent to "Nonsense!" Rustum's speech gives us some idea of the reasons for his anger with the king.

223. Kai Khosroo has been identified with Cyrus the Great, who lived about 500 B.C. In placing the story of Sohrab and Rustum in his reign, Arnold has varied the statement of the *Shah Nameh*, which put the incident during the reign of the "weak and brainless monarch" Kai Kaoos. Can you assign any reason for such a change?

230. Note the "dramatic irony" of this remark. See lines 609–11.

233. Modern Afghanistan includes ancient Seistan, where Zal lived.

242–8. Note how, when other means fail, the sneer of Gudurz moves Rustum to fight. For a somewhat similar situation, see *Julius Cæsar*, II. 2. 96–104.

257. in plain arms: with no device on the shield. This is an allusion to the custom of emblazoning the shields of knights with mottoes and devices. The method is well illustrated in Scott's *Ivanhoe*.

Why does Rustum make this decision? What is its effect upon the outcome of the conflict?

266. device: coat-of-arms, or other design by which he might be recognized.

270. In epic poetry, the horse of the hero plays an important part. Thus we have Xanthus, the horse of Achilles, in the *Iliad*. In the *Shah Nameh* we read that Rustum when a youth long sought a horse to carry him on his adventures. He tried many in vain, and at last, near Cabool, found a "rose-colored" steed of marvelous strength who had allowed no one to mount him until his pre-ordained master, Rustum, appeared. It was predicted that Rustum, mounted on Ruksh, would save the world.

Arnold, while preserving the spirit of the old epic, has somewhat simplified the story at this point.

288. **tale**: amount, number. Cf. Milton, *L'Allegro*, lines 67–8:

> "And every shepherd tells his tale,
> Under the hawthorn in the dale."

306. **flowers**: decorates with "frost-flowers."

311. **perused**: studied, watched closely.

314–8. Arnold was careful to select Eastern imagery in this passage. Hence, the "cypress, tall and dark and straight," and the "queen's secluded garden."

322. The conversation between heroes before they fight is common in epic poetry. Here, what is said adds greatly to the dramatic effect of the poem. Arnold has followed the *Shah Nameh* very closely at this point.

326. **tried**: experienced, tested by battle.

330. **governed**: persuaded.

331. Effective dramatic irony. Cf. lines 229, 447, 708–10.

343. **by thy father's head**, etc.: Such expressions are common in the impassioned language of the East.

345. **askance**: doubtfully, suspiciously.

367. **vaunt**: boast.

397. Cf. *Julius Cæsar*, V. 1. 123–6:

> "O, that a man might know
> The end of this day's business, ere it come;
> But it sufficeth that the day will end,
> And then the end is known."

401. **towered**: poised.

412. **Hyphasis or Hydaspes**: rivers of the Punjab in Northern India. The modern names are Jhelum and Beas.

414. **wrack**: wreckage, ruin.

418. **glancing**: gleaming in swift movement.

436–47. The pathetic appeal of Sohrab increases the tragic power of the poem.

452. **that autumn star**: Sirius, supposed by the ancients to cause epidemic diseases. It is also called the Dog Star and is the most brilliant fixed star in the heavens.

453. **baleful**: foreboding evil.

454. **crest**: helmet and plume.

455. **twice his voice**, etc.: Cf. *Paradise Lost*, I. 619–21:

> " Thrice he essayed, and thrice in spite of scorn,
> Tears such as angels weep burst forth : at last
> Words interwove with sighs found out their way."

458. **minion**: women's darling.

470. In the *Shah Nameh* the conflict is not confined to one day; Sohrab and Rustum contend three times. The first day's battle is ended by the approach of night. In order to increase the rapidity of the action and to heighten its dignity, Arnold has compressed the three battles into a single combat.

Why do you suppose he thus modified the original?

536. **glad**: make happy.

556–75. This is one of the most beautiful similes in English poetry.

563. **sole**: alone.

570. **glass**: reflect.

577. **prate**: foolish talk.

590. **my mother**: etc., Sohrab's mother was Tamineh, a Tartar princess. The *Shah Nameh* tells us that she was enamored of Rustum from hearing of his knightly deeds. On one occasion her emissaries stole Ruksh and led him away to Ader-baijan while Rustum was asleep. When he awoke, the hero tracked his horse to Samenegan, capital of Turan. He was met by the king, anxious to honor so distinguished a visitor. Rustum refused the proffered hospitality and demanded his horse. The king promised to return Ruksh, and while search was being made Rustum accepted the royal hospitality. Meantime Tamineh's maidens arranged for a meeting between their mistress and Rustum. Eventually they

were married, but shortly after the nuptials Rustum, as has been already related, was summoned by the king to lead important campaigns. It is worthy of note in this connection that in the Orient a strong attachment to the mother is universal.

596. **bruited up**: spread abroad, noised abroad.

613. **style**: name, or title.

625. **her father**: that is, the king of Samenegan.

626. **His wandering guest** was Rustum.

632. Like his own son would have been.

658–60. Here Arnold has again modified the story of the *Shah Nameh*, which says that Rustum gave Tamineh an onyx as an amulet to be given to their child as a means of identification. For this is substituted, in Arnold's poem, the seal pricked (tattooed) on Sohrab's arm. Can you give the reasons for making such a change?

664. **corslet**: breastplate.

672. **cunning**: skillful, deft.

679. **griffin**: the marvelous Simurgh that cared for Zal when his father left him to die on the mountain. See note on line 82.

700–701. Casting dust on one's head was the Eastern fashion of expressing deep grief or humiliation.

708–15. The first part of Sohrab's speech is a good example of that "fatalism" which is so characteristic of Eastern thought. The *Rubaiyat* of Omar Khayyam, a Persian poet of the twelfth century, is strongly marked by this spirit. The following lines are typical:

> " The moving finger writes, and having writ
> Moves on: nor all your piety nor wit
>   Shall lure it back to cancel half a line,
> Nor all your tears wash out a word of it."

Other examples of fatalism are seen in lines 387–97, 836–7.

710. **unconscious hand**: In the *Shah Nameh:*

> " Such is my destiny, such is the will of fortune.
> It was decreed that I should perish by the hand of my father."

722–5. In the *Shah Nameh:*

> " I came like a flash of lightning, and now I depart like the wind."

Cf. Job VII. 7:

> " O remember that my life is wind; mine eyes shall see no more good."

751. **Helmund**: a river of Afghanistan.

752. **Zirrah**: a lake in Afghanistan, now almost dry.

763–4. **Moorghab, Tejend, Kohik**: rivers of Turkestan, which lose their waters in the great desert south of Bokhara.

765. **the northern Sir**: the Jaxartes River.

783–9. The *Shah Nameh* tells us that all Sohrab's wishes were carried out. A thousand horses were sacrificed; then a great procession led by the chiefs bore the body to Seistan. When the funeral rites were concluded, the corpse was covered with a yellow robe and placed in a bier of aloes. Above the dead youth was raised a sepulchral mound, "formed like a charger's hoof." The last sixty lines of the episode in the original poem are devoted to a description of Tamineh's grief for her lost son.

815–7. With this, compare David's lament for Absalom, II Samuel XVIII, 33.

"And the king was much moved, and went up to the chamber over the gate, and wept: and as he wept, thus he said, O my son Absalom, my son, my son Absalom! would God I had died for thee, O Absalom, my son, my son!"

830–4. Kai Khosroo after Afrasiab's death determined to spend the rest of his days in retirement. He therefore divided his kingdom among his nobles, and with a few attendants went to a spring fixed upon as the place of his rest. Then he suddenly disappeared, and all who went with him were drowned on the return voyage. From the words of Sohrab in these lines we should infer that Rustum was among those who perished. But according to the *Shah Nameh* the great champion was killed through the wiles of his brother Shugdad when they were on a hunting expedition.

861. **Jemshid** was a mythical Persian king, whose glory and misfortune were a constant theme of the Persian poets.

Persepolis was the ancient capital of Persia, the seat of Jemshid.

866. **sole**: lonely.

878. **Chorasmian waste**: a desert region of Turkestan, now known as Khorassim.

880. **Right for the polar star**: that is, due north.

Orgunjé is a small village on the Oxus about 70 miles below Khiva, and situated at the head of the river delta.

890. **luminous home**: the shining spaces of the Aral Sea.

891. **new-bathed stars**: As the stars rise above the horizon of the sea, they appear to have come up out of the water.

875–92. In these closing lines, Arnold has given two beautiful pictures. One shows the great hosts going about their routine work and taking their evening meal; the other, the majestic Oxus flowing on unmoved by the tragedy just enacted on its banks. The artistic value of such an ending is important. It throws into high relief the passions of anger and grief which have gone before, and it leaves with the reader an impression of the inevitable march of fate. Such endings are characteristic of the author's works — peace after pain, rest after the turbulent passions of life.

TYPICAL PASSAGES FROM SOHRAB AND RUSTUM.

Through the black Tartar tents he passed, which stood
Clustering like bee-hives on the low flat strand
Of Oxus, where the summer floods o'erflow
When the sun melts the snow in high Pamere.

In the country, on a morn in June,
When the dew glistens on the pearled ears,
A shiver runs through the deep corn for joy.

Dear as the wet diver to the eyes
Of his pale wife who waits and weeps on shore,
By sandy Bahrein, in the Persian Gulf
Plunging all day in the blue waves, at night,
Having made up his tale of precious pearls
Rejoins her in their hut upon the sands.

The poor drudge
Who with numb blackened fingers makes her fire, —
At cock-crow, on a star-lit winter morn,
When the frost flowers the whitened window-panes.

Like some young cypress, tall and dark and straight,
Which in a queen's secluded garden throws
Its slight dark shadow on the moonlit turf,
By midnight, to a bubbling fountain's sound.

His giant figure planted on the sand,
Sole, like some single tower, which a chief
Hath builded on the waste in former years
Against the robbers.

For we are all, like swimmers in the sea,
Poised on the top of a huge wave of fate,
Which hangs uncertain to which side to fall.

As when some hunter in the spring hath found
A breeding eagle sitting on her nest,
Upon the craggy isle of a hill-lake,
And pierced her with an arrow as she rose,
And followed her to find her where she fell
Far off ; anon her mate comes winging back
From hunting, and a great way off descries
His huddling young left sole ; at that, he checks
His pinion, and with short uneasy sweeps
Circles above his eyry, with loud screams
Chiding his mate back to her nest ; but she
Lies dying, with the arrow in her side,
In some far stony gorge out of his ken,
A heap of fluttering feathers, — never more
Shall the lake glass her, flying over it ;
Never the black and dripping precipices
Echo her stormy scream as she sails by.
For he remembered his own early youth,
And all its bounding rapture ; as, at dawn,
The shepherd from his mountain-lodge descries
A far, bright city, smitten by the sun,
Through many rolling clouds.

As a cunning workman, in Pekin,
Pricks with vermillion some clear porcelain vase,
An emperor's gift, — at early morn he paints,
And all day long, and, when night comes, the lamp
Lights up his studious forehead and thin hands.

But the majestic river floated on,
Out of the mist and hum of that low land,

Into the frosty starlight, and there moved,
Rejoicing, through the hushed Chorasmian waste,
Under the solitary moon; he flowed
Right for the polar star, past Orgunjé,
Brimming, and bright, and large.

QUESTIONS AND TOPICS FOR DISCUSSION BASED ON SOHRAB AND RUSTUM.

1. Why did Arnold call his poem an " episode "?
2. What characteristics of epic poetry are found in the poem?
3. To what extent has the author departed from the original story as told in the *Shah Nameh?* What is gained by these modifications?
4. Arnold's method of supplying the antecedent information necessary to a full understanding of the story.
5. Comment upon the use of proper names.
6. What do you understand by " fatalism "? At what points in the poem is it suggested? What effect is gained thereby?
7. What is meant by " local color "? Show how Arnold employs this device to increase the effectiveness of his poem.
8. What dramatic effect is gained by the conversation between Sohrab and Rustum before the fight?
9. What means are employed by Arnold to intensify the pathos of Sohrab's death?
10. A critic has spoken of the " classic clearness and restraint " of Arnold's verse. Show how these qualities are manifested in *Sohrab and Rustum.*
11. In what respects is the quality of Arnold's poetry heightened by the use of simile and metaphor? Select two or three instances which seem to you especially appropriate.
12. Write a careful criticism of the opening and closing passages — lines 1–4, and lines 875–92. Wherein are they themselves effective, and how do they add to the artistic quality of the poem?
13. Explain, or comment upon, the following:
The black Tartar tents. High Pamere. Felts. An old man's sleep. The conquering Tartar ensigns. In Seistan, with Zal,

his father old. Dim is the rumor of a common fight. Some
frore Caspian reed-bed. Aloof he sits. Kai Khosroo. With
my great name fence that weak old man. The baleful sign of
fevers. Curled minion. That seal which Rustum to my
mother gave. Thou art Heaven's unconscious hand. It was
writ in Heaven that this should be. By Jemshid in Persepolis. The hushed Chorasmian waste. The shorn and parcelled Oxus.

ENOCH ARDEN.

Enoch Arden was first published in 1864 in a volume entitled
Enoch Arden and Other Poems. It is a story of humble joys and
sorrows, like some of the tales told fifty and sixty years earlier by
Crabbe and Wordsworth. The subject was not new; many such
occurrences must have taken place in the old sailing-ship days.
The adventures of shipwrecked mariners have made themes for
many writers of prose and verse ever since Robinson Crusoe was
cast away on his island. The essentially original part of *Enoch
Arden* lies in the close, which differs materially from the usual end
ing where the wanderer returns to be welcomed, or to claim his
rights, and " lives happily ever after." Tennyson prefers the note
of pathos and of noble self-sacrifice.

Of the origin of his poem the poet wrote : "*Enoch Arden* (like
Aylmer's Field) is founded on a theme given me by the sculptor
Woolner. I believe that this particular story came out of Suffolk,
but something like the same story is told in Brittany and elsewhere."
The poem is well suited to Tennyson's genius, and shows his characteristic power to present pictures that are full of light and color
and vivid detail. He aimed to write a quiet unadorned narrative;
the note has been kept low, while the humanity of the situation is
conceived with full power. Thus, in the end Arden rises superior
to fate. He might have died a weakling, but he conquers his misery
and even after the realization of his sorrow is " not all unhappy."

For the most part the poem is marked by extreme simplicity of
structure. Some of the critics have said, however, that the descriptive passages are too ornate for so plain a tale — that the
poem, in a word, is loaded down with ornament. Whether or not

this be true (and it is to a large extent a matter for personal judgment), *Enoch Arden* has always been popular and few of Tennyson's poems are more widely read to-day. It has been dramatized, and translated at various times into seven European languages. Indeed, for clearness of outline, sincerity of feeling, and straight-forwardness of language, it ranks among the best of Tennyson's poems of English life.

1–9. It is well to note, from the very first, Tennyson's power of making every word count. His command of the effective phrase — the " inevitable word " — appears over and over again in this poem, as it does in everything he wrote. In this opening passage there is not a word thrown away, not a line wasted. The effect is extraordinarily vivid. Other sections which show the mastery of language and the fruits of close and accurate observation may be indicated : lines 15–18, 91–100, 129–31, 375–80, 537–46, 568–95, 605–8, 654–7.

The first lines of the poem describe a little seaport on the east coast of England. The scene is typical, with the single long street climbing to the downs at the cliff-top, the clustered houses, and the ancient church.

5. So the land would appear to one looking up from the village.

7. **Danish barrows**: funeral mounds. The Danes invaded England in the ninth and tenth centuries and for a time held all the eastern coast. It was their custom to erect great " barrows " on the cliffs to their dead. Even to-day some remains of these barrows may be traced.

10. The **hundred years** would of course place the date of the story at about 1760–1800. Why does Tennyson set it in the past rather than in the present?

36. This is an unconscious prophecy. The supernatural element enters into the poem in several places. The prophecies, Annie's dream, and her reliance upon the passage in the Bible (490–506) to shape her decision, make the story seem more true to the life of the simple-minded fisher-folk.

54. **full sailor**: as we should say, " able seaman."

67–8. That is, just where the hazel-wood began to grow down the slope of the hollow.

80–1. This is an example of " onomatopœia " — the use of sound to imitate the sense. The melody of these lines helps to picture the joyfulness presented by the words. Cf. lines 507–8

94. **ocean-smelling osier** : basket smelling of the sea.

96. **market-cross** : Many towns and villages had a cross erected conspicuously in the market-place.   From its steps public announcements were made, and around it on market-days the principal trading took place.   The cross was in various ways the center of village life.

98. **portal-warding lion-whelp** : the carved stone lions at the gate-entrance to the Hall, or residence of the nobleman of the county.

99. **peacock yew tree** : the yew tree was trimmed to the shape of a peacock.   Such treatment of the evergreen trees is common in English formal gardens.   A beautiful description of such a garden is found in Kipling's story, *They*.

100. **Friday fare** : fish was usually eaten on Fridays, in accordance with a custom of the church.   The whole passage, lines 92–100, has been commented on as being too highly decorative.   One critic remarked : " So much has not often been made of selling fish." What is your own opinion ?

110. A competitor was taking his work in his absence.

131. **isles a light in the offing** : lets the sun shine on a single spot far out at sea, the rest of the scene being momentarily darkened. This is a common phenomenon in cloudy weather on the coast, but the expression of it here is wonderfully condensed and accurate.

154. **appraised** : guessed.

167. **bore it thro'** : carried out his purpose.

168. **his old sea-friend** : his fishing-boat.

174–5. A touch of warning ; it suggests future trouble.

177. **order'd** : arranged carefully.

186. **that mystery** : of prayer.   See the beautiful lines in *The Passing of Arthur* :

> " More things are wrought by prayer
> Than this world dreams of. . . .
> For what are men better than sheep or goats
> That nourish a blind life within the brain,
> If, knowing God, they lift not hands of prayer
> Both for themselves and those who call them friend ?
> For thus the whole round earth is every way
> Bound by gold chains about the feet of God."

205–9. Tennyson considered this one of the tenderest similes he had written. Of the similes in this poem in general, he said that he thought they were all such as might have naturally been used by plain seafaring people.

210–12. Another unconscious prophecy.

218–26. Enoch's parting words are simple and manly, quite typical of the man. Note how his language reflects both his sailor's life and his honest and truthful religious feeling. For the Biblical quotations, see I Peter V, 7; Hebrews VI, 19; Psalms CXXXIX, 7, 9–10; XCV, 5.

247. **to chime with his** : to do as he wished.

265–6. Lack of money to pay the doctor.

285. **passion** : deep grief.

326. **garth** : garden, an obsolete word of Anglo-Saxon origin. See also line 671. Tennyson was fond of these old-fashioned, but very expressive words, and revived a number of them in his poetry.

337. **conies** : rabbits.

339. **To save the offence of charitable** : To avoid offending her by appearing to give through mere charity.

364. **Blanch'd with his mill** : whitened with flour-dust.

370–1. Cf. lines 67–8. Do you see the significance of this repetition?

376. **the whitening hazels** : the light-colored under side of the hazel-leaves are turned upwards as the children plunge through.

444–7. The poet brings out here the fine quality of Philip's consideration for Annie.

457–9. What impression of Annie's character do you gain from these lines?

470. Annoyance that their calculations had turned out wrong.

491–3. The method of divination used by Annie is known as "Sortes Biblicæ," or "Bibliomancy." The Bible is opened at random and the first passage that is touched by the finger is supposed to give the desired information. The Greeks and Romans applied in the same way to the poetry of Homer and Vergil. Bibliomancy was much used by the Puritans, and belief in its efficacy may still be found in remote parts of England and Scotland.

494. Cf. Judges IV, 5.

502. Cf. St. John XII, 13 ; St. Matthew XXI, 9 ; St. Mark XI, 10.

506. **So : if.** The usage is peculiar, though found elsewhere in Tennyson's poems. With the future or subjunctive " so " is equivalent to " if," or " provided that."

507–9. These lines form a good example of Tennyson's metrical skill. The first two (as in 80–1), are onomatopoetic; the rapid movement indicates the joyful ringing. The change of feeling is suggested in line 509 by the changed accent of " merrily."

510–16. With this mysterious instinct, compare the presentiment in lines 174–5, and 609–12.

523–33, 537–49. These passages show Tennyson's power as an interpreter of the sea. Other examples may be found in *The Merman, The Sailor Boy, The Revenge, The Voyage, Sea Dreams.*

525. **the Biscay :** the Bay of Biscay, notorious for rough weather.

528. **long tumble about the Cape :** The usual route to India and China in those days was round the Cape of Good Hope. Here sailors invariably met the " roaring forties " — the tremendous seas of those southerly latitudes.

565. **Fire-hollowing,** etc. : burning out the log to make a canoe, after the fashion of the Indians.

568–95. Although Tennyson longed all his life to visit the tropics, he never had an opportunity of doing so. Travelers have borne witness, however, to the undeniable truth and beauty of the picture of a tropical island here unfolded. The whole passage was one which the poet liked to read aloud.

568. **lawns :** open spaces. Cf. *The Vision of Sin :*

> " As when the sun, a crescent of eclipse,
>   Dreams over lake and lawn, and isles and capes."

Compare also Milton, *L'Allegro :*

> " Russet lawns, and fallows gray,
>   Where the nibbling flocks do stray."

and Moore, *Echoes :*

> " How sweet the answer Echo makes
>   To Music at night ;
>   When, roused by lute or horn, she wakes
>   And far away o'er lawns and lakes
>   Goes answering light ! "

570. **coco's**: the cocoa-nut tree.

580. In this line the poet imitates the surge of the sea. Kipling has a somewhat similar passage in his *The English Flag:*

" The long-backed breakers croon
Their endless ocean legends to the lazy, locked lagoon."

593. In allusion to the apparent size of the stars, as seen in the tropics.

594. An instance of close observation. It is a fact that the roar of the surf seems to grow louder as the night goes on. For a like thought, see *The Valley of Cauterez:*

" All along the valley, stream that flashest white,
Deepening thy voice with the deepening of the night. . . ."

The closing lines (587–95) make a fine summary of the loneliness and the splendor which surrounded the shipwrecked man.

601. **the line**: the Equator.

602–8. Note the strong contrast to the picture of the island.

609–13. The mysterious sympathy through which Enoch heard the far-distant pealing of the bells for Annie's marriage is another touch of the supernatural. The poet had warrant for what he wrote. " Mr. Kinglake told me," he said, " that he heard his own parish bells in the desert on a Sunday morning when they would have been ringing at home: and added, ' I might have had a singing in my ears, and the imaginative memory did the rest.' " For a description of a somewhat similar thought communication, see *Aylmer's Field*, lines 578 ff. Other instances will be found in *The Lover's Tale, Rizpah,* and *The Wreck.*

627. **since**: here, " because."

640–1. Cf. St. Mark, VII, 35; St. Luke, I, 64.

649. **his country**: his part of the country.

657. **her ghostly wall**: the fog-wreathed cliffs; or, the familiar white cliffs of the southern coast — " the white cliffs of old England."

659. Took up a collection for him.

665–75. A singularly effective picture of the coming of a sea-fog. Any one who has lived in a seaport will realize the fidelity of the description.

What was Tennyson's purpose in suggesting this change in the appearance of nature?

671. **holt**: group of trees; **tilth**: tilled fields. See note on 326.

688. **timber-crost antiquity**: In the older type of building, the supporting beams were frequently carried up outside the walls.

698. **annals**: past happenings.

715–6. Cf. *The Passing of Arthur*:

> " His own thought drove him like a goad."

724–6. Cf. Longfellow, *The Lighthouse*:

> " The sea-bird wheeling round it, with the din
> Of wings and wind and melancholy cries,
> Blinded and maddened by the glare within
> Dashes himself against the glare, and dies."

733. **shingle**: large pebbles. In England a " shingle " beach means one composed of stones larger than the ordinary pebble.

762. A truth which is powerfully enforced by the setting.

776–87. If Tennyson had been morbid, or sentimental, he would have had the long-lost husband meet his wife, and thus have spoiled the artistic effect of the tragedy. As it is, the poem ends upon a note of noble self-sacrifice.

803. **enow**: enough — an obsolete form.

812. **tall barks**: Cf. Masefield, *Sea Fever*:

> " All I ask is a tall ship,
> And a star to steer her by."

813. **stinted commerce**: lessened trade.

834. **swear upon the book**: on the Bible, which of course made the oath more binding.

842. **far away**: long ago.

860–4. An excellent characterization of the talkative and uneducated country-woman.

870–97. Besides the deepest pathos, there is real nobility of thought in these last words of Enoch Arden. We both pity the speaker and respect him. " There is . . . something profoundly sad in the way in which that desolate heart, after half claiming back the living children, feels that, in real fact, only the dead little one is left it."

897–901. Another interesting bit of characterization. The first two lines imitate by their sound the chatter of Miriam Lane.

904. **a calling of the sea** : Tennyson said of this expression : " The calling of the sea is a term used, I believe, chiefly in the Western parts of England, to signify a ground swell. When this occurs on a windless night, the echo of it rings through the timbers of the old houses in a haven."

911. **a costlier funeral** : A sound knowledge of human nature is shown by the choice of the word " costlier." Can you explain why Tennyson used it?

TYPICAL PASSAGES FROM ENOCH ARDEN.

> He thrice had plucked a life
> From the dread sweep of the down-streaming seas.

> His face
> Rough-reddened with a thousand winter gales.

> Some little cloud
> Cuts off the fiery highway of the sun,
> And isles a light in the offing.

> As the village girl,
> Who sets her pitcher underneath the spring
> Musing on him who used to fill it for her,
> Hears and not hears, and lets it overflow.

> The lazy gossip of the port.

> Faint as a figure seen at early dawn
> Down at the far end of an avenue.

> A seaward-gazing mountain gorge.

> The myriad shriek of wheeling ocean-fowl,
> The league-long roller thundering on the reef,
> The moving whisper of huge trees that branch'd
> And blossom'd in the zenith, or the sweep
> Of some precipitous rivulet to the wave.
> The sunrise broken into scarlet shafts
> Among the palms and ferns and precipices.

       The chill
November dawns and dewy-glooming downs,
The gentle shower, the smell of dying leaves,
And the low moan of leaden-color'd seas.

       The mate had seen at early dawn
Across a break on the mist-wreathen isle.
The silent water slipping from the hills.

       The dewy meadowy morning-breath
Of England, blown across her ghostly wall.

       Thro' the dripping haze
The dead weight of the dead leaf bore it down.

The ruddy square of comfortable light,
Far-blazing from the rear of Philip's house.

There came so loud a calling of the sea,
That all the houses in the haven rang.

QUESTIONS AND TOPICS FOR DISCUSSION BASED ON ENOCH ARDEN.

1. Before *Enoch Arden* was written, a friend of Tennyson's said: "Alfred wants a story to treat, being full of poetry with nothing to put it in." In reading the poem, are you more impressed by the "story," or by the "poetry"?
2. Make a list of picturesque phrases found in the poem.
3. Make a list of the unusual or archaic words, and comment upon their poetic value.
4. "Ornate," and "decorative," are epithets sometimes applied to Tennyson's style. Discuss their appropriateness as applied to *Enoch Arden*. Use quotations to illustrate what you say.
5. Select two or three descriptive passages which seem to you typical of the author. Comment upon their characteristic features.
6. Pick out some instances of the poet's close observation of nature.

7. Comment upon the characters of Enoch, Philip, and Annie, as these are developed in the poem.

8. Write an explanatory comment upon the following statement:
"There is no excess or defect of any human passion that might have worked his doom for any. Here no one sins except life itself; and for the evil of bare human life Nemesis may in some sense be reserved."

9. Judging by this poem, should you say that Tennyson was more successful in his interpretation of domestic life, or in his descriptions of scenery?

10. The elements of pathos and tragedy, as employed in the closing portion of the poem — lines 622–911.

11. Explain, or comment upon, the following:
Danish barrows. Anchors of rusty fluke. The prone edge of the wood. Had his dark hour unseen. The market-cross. Isles a light in the offing. His old sea-friend. That mystery where God-in-man is one with man-in-God. The little garth. Conies from the down. Abhorrent of a calculation crossed. Long tumble about the Cape. Blossomed in the zenith. The hollower-bellowing ocean. His long-bounden tongue. Holt or tilth or pasturage. Timber-crost antiquity. A calling of the sea.

GENERAL QUESTIONS AND TOPICS FOR DISCUSSION.

1. Compare the blank verse of *Sohrab and Rustum* and *Enoch Arden*. What seem to you the characteristics of each type? In what respects does each reflect the literary qualities of the author?

2. Which of the three poems shows the highest imaginative power? The greatest beauty of language? The closest knowledge of nature? The deepest pathos? The clearest analysis of character? Illustrate what you say by quotations.

3. "There is a simplicity of manner in each of the poems; but the simplicity while in each case appropriate, is in each case distinctive."
Write an explanatory comment upon this statement.

4. From what you know of the lives of the three poets, indicate to what extent their lives influenced their poetry.

5. Select a typical descriptive passage from each poem. Give careful reasons for your choice.

6. Which of the three poems is in your opinion most satisfactory as a piece of narrative writing? Most beautiful as a poem?

7. Make a detailed comparative study of the following passages:
   The Ancient Mariner, lines 358–372.
   Sohrab and Rustum, lines 556–572.
   Enoch Arden, lines 568–595.

8. Compare the sea-pictures in *The Ancient Mariner* with those in *Enoch Arden.* Discuss, from the point of view of truth to life and imaginative quality.

9. What do you understand by the " atmosphere " of a poem? What methods are employed by each author to create an atmosphere?

10. Compare, or contrast, the opening of the poems. In each case, comment upon the purpose which the author had in view.

11. Compare, or contrast, the closing portions of the poems. What special methods are employed by each author to attain his purpose? Consider both the thought and the expression.

12. Write a note upon the following aids to poetic effect, as you find them in the poems under discussion:
    Simile. Metaphor. Onomatopœia. Climax.

10 similes — as, like
What is compared with what.

Irony (3)
Fat ahism (3)